THAT
*OF*
*Hope*

# THAT SEASON
## OF
# *Hope*

## A TRUE STORY

A TEAM.
A CITY.
A GIRL'S LAST WISH.
## ONE BEAUTIFUL BLUR.

# KEITH LARSON
## WITH NANCY LARSON

**TATE PUBLISHING**
AND ENTERPRISES, LLC

Published by Tate Publishing & Enterprises, LLC
127 E. Trade Center Terrace | Mustang, Oklahoma 73064 USA
1.888.361.9473 | www.tatepublishing.com

Tate Publishing is committed to excellence in the publishing industry. The company reflects the philosophy established by the founders, based on Psalm 68:11,
*"The Lord gave the word and great was the company of those who published it."*

Book design copyright © 2013 by Tate Publishing, LLC. All rights reserved.
*Cover design by Kendall M. Larson*
*Interior design by Mary Jean Archival*

Published in the United States of America

ISBN: 978-1-62902-766-1
1. Family & Relationships / Family Relationships
2. Sports & Recreation / Football
13.08.29

Hope—
I'm sorry this took so long.

This is dedicated also to my son, Matt,
and daughters, Hallie and Kendall,
who have each inspired me to finish what you start.

# PREFACE

I HAD WRITTEN a *profound* preface for this book. It was about how book prefaces make a writer look brilliant and insightful but are really "cheats" because the author is usually writing the preface last, after the entire book is written. This is when he has the advantage of knowing all and is able to sit back, ponder, and pack the essence of his story, his journey, and his winks and nods and tip-offs into a few paragraphs or pages. These will foreshadow the book's tale and equip you with context, meaning, and outcomes – or veiled hints at them. My fabulous preface about prefaces was its own allegory because I had actually written it *before* writing my book. My wink and nod was that life doesn't come with a preface; doesn't give you a few paragraphs or pages to read up front that foreshadow its tale and equip you with context, meaning, and outcomes, or even veiled hints at them. I wrote:

*Rarely do we see coming the days that will change our lives. For Hope, Shelby, and Stuart Stout, it turned out to be Friday, June 27, 2003. For Jake Delhomme, Sunday, September 7, 2003. For Kevin Donnalley, Sunday, October 19. For me, it was Friday, December 19, 2003.*

*Maybe this will be your December 19.*

Thing is, it wasn't true. Oh, it was true that those days had changed the lives of Hope Stout and her family, Jake, Kevin, and me, and we hadn't seen them coming; but it wasn't true that I had written this book to make that profound point. Pat Conroy broke that news to me.

I don't worship at the altar of Southern Writers, the way so many writers from the South do, but my friend Molly Grantham does. She's an effective evangelist for all to which she is faithful, and so for Christmas one year, *The Water is Wide*; for my birthday another, *My Losing Season*. Those two works comprise the full extent of my Conroy experience, and in truth, I am as I write this, almost but not yet, done with *Season*. I had begun reading the birthday gift a few months after it was given. Most of the way through his book, Conroy tells of his 1966 Citadel basketball team's epic four-overtime defeat of its archrival VMI, the Virginia Military Institute. Recounting the game propels him into an emotional remembrance of a member of the team killed in Vietnam the following year, and then into a fantasized conversation between Conroy, the best-selling fiction writer, and his recollection of Conroy, the Citadel Bulldogs' point guard.

"How'd you like the game?" the author asks the 21-year-old point guard.

"Your wife's right, you don't actually write fiction."

"There was no reason to change it," Conroy, the author, explains to his imagined young self. "The game was perfect. I'd never felt that way before or since. I wanted the reader to know how it felt."

That sentence rocked me. Maybe because I was reading alone on a chilly, gray Saturday morning. Or maybe because I had been in the throes of the desperate, hopeful, hopelessness of trying to get a first book published.

No.

It rocked me because it was, among all the truths I had known and feelings I had felt in writing my own book, the truest feeling of all. Conroy's sentence pierced instantly that same truth as it lived silently in fear of still-birth, deep inside my heart.

I had started writing about Hope and her wish and the Carolina Panthers' improbable run to the Super Bowl not long after the game. I was fired up and committed, but before long, put the pen down and the project off for several years for certain specific reasons that are not important now. But it never left me. Never even wandered.

That season of Hope lives inside me and breaks me open with a joy and heartache and love like none I have ever known; like nothing I could ever have imagined. It was a love story of a city, a football team, and a dying girl and her last wish. Yet it wasn't a *story* – it was *real*. It all happened. I want you to know about it. I want you to know how it felt.

It is now 9:04 a.m. on Saturday, March 2, 2013. When Conroy jumped me an hour ago, I was consumed by the fire of how much I wanted you to know how it felt, no matter what I had to do to get the story to you.

We rarely do see coming the days that will change our lives. I didn't see Pat Conroy or March 2, 2013 coming, either.

# CONTENTS

# THAT SEASON OF HOPE

# PART I

# CHAPTER 1

# THE PANTHERS

SINCE THEIR STORYBOOK first two seasons, the Carolina Panthers had been a swirling mess. They were born into the National Football League in 1995 and made the best debut ever for an expansion team. They won seven games and lost nine their first year, but that was nothing compared to their second. The '96 Panthers went 12-4. They made the playoffs, won their division, and fell one game short of going to the Super Bowl, losing to the eventual champion Green Bay Packers. It was a thrilling start to life in the NFL for the Panthers, for team owner Jerry Richardson, and for millions of fans throughout the Carolinas.

The thrill didn't last long.

They fell to 7-9 the next season, and tumbled to 4-12 the year after that. A change in head coaches led to an 8-8 record in 1999, but the Panthers slipped back to 7-9 in 2000.

To open 2001, the Panthers traveled to Minnesota, to the famously loud and infamously visiting-team-hostile Metrodome, and beat the Vikings 24-13. It was the last game they would win all year. Fifteen straight losses followed. The young team that shot to the conference championship game in only its sophomore year had plummeted to the worst record in the league, and the worst losing streak in the history of the league, only five years later. As the wins disappeared, so did the fans. The 72,000-seat stadium that was regularly packed and was *the place to be* in Charlotte only a few years earlier, now had twice as many seats empty as filled. As the wins and the fans disappeared, so did another head coach.

John Fox was hired in 2002. Disciplined and reserved, Fox had been defensive coordinator for the New York Giants and brought with him a classically conservative NFL approach: win by not losing, use the running game to drive the offense and live off your defense. It wasn't flashy, but it was what the Panthers needed. In their first season under Fox, the previously 1-15 Panthers improved to 7-9.

The four-game NFL pre-season means nothing. Unless you go 4-0 and beat the likes of the Washington Redskins, New York Giants, Green Bay Packers, and Pittsburgh Steelers. Then it means something. And what it meant in 2003, when the last weekend of August turned into the first weekend of September and the exhibition season turned into the real thing, was that the Carolina Panthers were not supposed to be getting shut out by the Jacksonville Jaguars.

Sunday, September 7, was gray, drizzling, and thickly warm in Charlotte, and the Panthers were as dismal as the day. They were down 17-0 in the third quarter. Rodney Peete, a solid if not spectacular, NFL quarterback, was in his fifteenth year in the league and his second with the Panthers. He was picked up after the miserable 1-15 season for his experience and maturity and was all the quarterback John Fox needed to start the Panthers turn-around and win those seven games in 2002. But Peete didn't have it opening day 2003. By halftime he had completed only four passes for a total of 19 yards, and the rest of the offense was following his listless lead. They had picked up only one first down the entire half, and the running game had managed only 17 yards. Pathetic.

John Fox is about as far from a hair-trigger guy as you're going to find as an NFL coach, but his gut told him there was far more at stake than strictly the game at hand. It wasn't just the lopsided score. In the first half of that first game of the season, the Carolina Panthers had the frightening look of a team that could actually, possibly, go worse than 1-15.

Change was needed—now. Fox had to turn around not just a game, but maybe a season. When the Panthers' offense took the field in the third quarter, he sent in Jake Delhomme for Rodney Peete.

TWENTY-EIGHT-YEAR-OLD Jake Christopher Delhomme, from Breaux Bridge, Louisiana, 100 miles west of New Orleans, had been knocking around trying to find a place in the National Football League for five years. He played his college ball for Louisiana-Lafayette and entered the pro football draft in 1997. NFL teams chose 253 players that year. Jake Christopher Delhomme was not one of them.

Undeterred, he talked his way into a tryout with his hometown New Orleans Saints and was signed; then was dumped two months later, before the season even started. Jake kept banging on the door and got hired onto the Saints' practice squad: the guys who get paid nearly nothing to take the field in workouts and get pummeled by the starters.

After the '97 season, Jake was sent by the Saints to the Amsterdam Admirals of the NFL's European league. So this *Loosiana Cajun* left the only state where he'd ever lived, left the sprawling metropolis of Breaux Bridge (population 5,000), left Keri Melancon, the girl he'd been dating since the seventh grade, and went bouncing around Europe trying to keep his dream of playing in the NFL alive.

New Orleans brought him home for the '98 season as their third backup. He lasted five games before being shipped off for another season in Europe. Back in New Orleans the next year, the Saints signed Jake again, but then cut him again.

Delhomme just wouldn't take the hint. Then again, neither did New Orleans.

The Saints re-signed him in November 1999 as third backup, and on Christmas Eve, Jake Delhomme finally got his first chance as a starting quarterback in the National Football League. He completed 16 of 27 passes for 278 yards and two touchdowns, ran for a touchdown himself, and led the Saints over the Dallas Cowboys for what was only their third win of the year. Jake was rewarded with three more years riding the bench as the Saints' backup. He only got on the field in four games.

Heading into 2003, Carolina's journeyman Rodney Peete, at 37, was getting old for a quarterback. The Panthers were scrambling for a number two; a guy who could maybe become a starter down the line. They took a chance and signed Delhomme, perhaps not in spite of his hardscrabble NFL history, but because of it: his determination, his hard work, his willingness to do whatever he had to. They thought they saw in him glimpses of a guy who could stand and deliver if he ever got the chance. He had done it at Louisiana-Lafayette, and he had done it in that first ever NFL start against Dallas.

The Panthers also saw in Jake a gushing love of football. He was 28-going-on-13, and he had energy and enthusiasm for football and for life that was contagious. It was beyond contagious. Jake Delhomme was an enthusiasm epidemic. The very businesslike Carolina Panthers – owned by a former NFL player turned successful businessman, based in acutely businesslike Charlotte, led by one of the most businesslike coaches in the league, John Fox – knew they needed a shot of something if they were going to rise above their painfully mediocre last five years. They thought Jake Delhomme, with his boyish grin, even more boyish haircut, and boyishly boundless energy, might be that something. That shot is what John Fox was desperately reaching for when he tapped Delhomme opening day after the Panthers' flaccid first thirty minutes.

HE RACED ONTO THE FIELD and smacked the hands and helmets of his ten disheartened offensive teammates as he jumped into the center of the huddle to call the play. "Okay, let's GO! Get your heads up! We can *DO* this!"

In his first series as quarterback of the Carolina Panthers, Jake Delhomme briskly marched the team 64 yards for a touchdown on four plays. He found reliable receiver Muhsin Muhammad with a pass over the middle for the score that launched Jake and 64,347 of his new best friends into the air in celebration.

On their next possession, Delhomme led the Panthers close enough for a John Kasay field goal, and when they got the ball back minutes later, Jake delivered again. This time he cranked out 52 yards in seven plays, finally hitting the explosive Steve Smith, who went airborne at the goal line to complete Delhomme's second touchdown pass. With six minutes left in the game and a two-point safety chipped in by the defense, the Panthers had grabbed the lead.

The stadium was rocking. The Panthers had played like they were hypnotized in the first half, but in the second, were snapped out of their stupor into a pepped-up, pumped-up football team by a quarterback who might just as easily have been a kid on an 1890s street corner with a newspaper bag shouting, "EXTRA, EXTRA READ ALL ABOUT

IT!" Still, the Jaguars weren't letting Jake go to press with a "COMEBACK!" headline just yet.

Down 18-17, Jacksonville snatched back the lead on a 65-yard touchdown pass. They tried a two-point conversion after the touchdown which would have given them a seven-point lead instead of going for the one-point conversion kick. The Panthers held tough and stopped them, leaving the Jaguars up by only five.

The Jacksonville scoring drive had been stunning and swift. Actually, too swift. It had run only 56 seconds off the clock. There were still more than five minutes left. In a game that had become an offensive shootout, each team's defense now showed up. The Jaguars shut the Panthers down, and the Panthers returned the favor. When Jacksonville punted, Steve Smith got the ball on his own 10-yard line and shot off on a 36-yard return that put Carolina almost at midfield, with three and a half minutes remaining. Plenty of time, everyone now knew, for Jake to put together a touchdown drive.

But could he? Was there one more march to the end zone still in the wrist bands of the Panthers' sudden new leader, the Ragin' Cajun Jake Delhomme, a guy most fans probably hadn't even heard of an hour earlier and whose name (Duh LOME) no one seemed to know how to pronounce? Could the kid out of nowhere bring the team from behind again? This time, for the win?

Jake and the Panthers rattled off eleven plays and plowed to the Jaguar 12-yard line. When receiver Ricky Proehl floated over a Jacksonville defender to snag a pass with sixteen seconds left and fell back to earth just inside the end zone for the touchdown, 28-going-on-13-year-old Jake Delhomme leaped into the air with waving arms and wild eyes, hooting and hollering at the top of his lungs. He ran and hugged

Proehl before sprinting back up the field, pumping both hands in celebration to an erupting Panther Stadium crowd.

As the gun rang out, the breathtaking, double-come-from-behind, 24-23 win over Jacksonville had tattooed itself on the hearts of fans. It turned opening day 2003 from an impending disaster into the greatest comeback in team history. It made Jake Delhomme look like a hero and John Fox look like a genius.

Rodney Peete never started another game in the National Football League.

# CHAPTER 2

# THE GIRL

SHE WOULD GROW UP wanting to be a movie star. Her entrance into the world on March 4, 1991, right on cue and with a surprising shock of fiery red hair, seemed as grand to Stuart and Shelby Stout as an actress materializing on stage to accept her Academy Award. Austin was six years old, and Holly three, when their baby sister Hope was born. Despite the tinge of strawberry in Stuart's blonde mop, neither of the older girls inherited the flaming red hair gene his family carried. It only occasionally sprang on the scene. There was no profound vision or intriguing back story in their choosing "Hope." Rather, Stuart and Shelby were stuck for a girl's name. In fact, they weren't even considering the possibility of a girl when they decided to have their third child. In a house with three women, Stuart was quite naturally wishing for a son, and Shelby was hoping for a boy this time as well. Stuart was an insurance consultant, though, and all about being prepared. So they set about choosing a girl's name too. Just in case.

They were stumped. They gave it their best shot time and again but were confounded by the challenge of figuring out another just-right name for a girl. They convened in their bedroom in yet another attempt to solve the riddle. Arriving at the same disheartening end as in previous efforts, they crashed into a moment of surrender. Stuart flopped on the bed and Shelby sat with her chin in her hands and her elbows on her knees on the wooden chest Stuart had given her before they were married. The large letters H-O-P-E were carved on its front.

Life's most profound visions and intriguing back stories are often the ones we don't even know are there until they want us to.

JUST AS HER DOWNY HAIR at birth wasn't merely reddish or even red but truly a *flaming* red, everything about Hope seemed to push the envelope. As a toddler, she didn't just drive around in her little Cozy Coupe, she drove with the passion of a Petty. She graduated to a tricycle and then a bicycle and as soon as Santa brought her one, an electric scooter. Santa knew to bring Hope's best friend, Emily Rutherford, a scooter that same Christmas too. That the wreck they got into didn't result in more than bumps and bruises for both girls, and twelve stitches on the right knee for Hope, was reported as miraculous by the witnesses.

The scooters made it easier for Hope and Emily to dash through the rolling streets of their rambling wooded neighborhood. The Rutherfords had moved in the summer before third grade and the girls became fast friends. They were curious, goofy, free-spirited girls. They loved to dress up even when it wasn't Halloween. Hope liked being one of the Spice Girls while Emily preferred being an M&M. They were good friends to others, too. Like, when backyard buddy, Zach Tompkins, was on vacation, they watched his cat. And somehow his backyard zip line ended up broken even though they weren't supposed to be playing on it. How were two curious, goofy, free-spirited girls supposed to resist a zip line? Its destruction at their hands remained their secret.

When Hope wasn't a Spice Girl to Emily's M&M, she was the Mary Kate to Gina Wheeling's Ashley Olsen. Gina had been Hope's other best friend since first grade. They were always cooking up adventures like the famous twins, posing as sisters themselves, and going by fake names. They loved pretending to be royalty and talked in British accents. They were both cheerleaders and made the squad together in sixth grade.

Hope didn't just lead cheers, she played sports too. She picked up softball from Austin, golf from Holly, and as for basketball – growing up in North Carolina with family all throughout N.C. State, Duke, Wake Forest, and University of North Carolina country – basketball was in Hope's DNA. If the four-inch growth spurt she'd had the past year left her at times feeling a little gangly, the 5-foot-6-inches with which she could now stride onto the basketball court had her itching to enter seventh grade so she could go out for the team.

And Hope loved football. She grew up on Carolina Panthers football, and the Panthers grew up right along with her. The game Stuart took Hope to on a hot August night in 1996, her very first, was also the very first game the Panthers played in their brand new stadium. It was a fabulous night in Charlotte. No one cared about the 88-degrees or the drenching humidity. Having been one of the original Panthers' season ticket holders, Stuart would be there, of course. He knew it would be the perfect introduction to the Panthers for his 5-year-old daughter.

She was decked out in the team's colors of blue, silver, and black. At a booth outside the stadium, she had gotten a snarling panther painted on her cheek. In her spirit colors, with the logo on her face and her head full of blazing red hair, little Hope was quite the sight as she climbed atop the base of one of the six giant bronze panthers guarding the main gates. The massive marble rectangles on which they rest are carved with the names of those first season ticket holders, and Hope wanted to see hers.

She was cautiously inching around the top edge of the monument in a way that made her a magnet for several fans taking in the celebration before the game. The scene caught the eye of a TV reporter and cameraman from Charleston, who were among several such crews trolling the grounds capturing the circus-like atmosphere. The reporter stepped up to interview the star of this center ring and Hope turned to the camera the moment its red light blinked.

"Hi there, what's your name?"

"Hope."

"Are you a Panther fan, Hope?"

"Yes."

"Aren't you afraid of *this* panther?"

"No.

"Well, why not? It's pretty big and ferocious-looking!"

"Because… *he's* not *real*."

Even at age five, Hope did not suffer those she thought foolish, gladly.

MAYBE PART OF HER CRUSH on the Carolina Panthers was the fact that her absolute favorite animals were kittens and cats. They always seemed to populate the Stout home.

Hope had two equally kitten-smitten sisters in Austin and Holly. They all had a cat-loving mentor in Shelby. And in Stuart, they had a father and husband whose heart was owned by those "FOURCHIX," as his license plate read. That's why, even though there were already two cats, Buffy and Abby, living in the Stout home along with their Dachshund, Daisy, Stuart didn't even pretend to fight when they called one day begging to adopt one of the new kitties born into the world by Shelby's brother's cat.

Buffy and Abby were joined by the new kitten the girls named Baby. Now there were three cats living in the Stout home along with Stuart, his FOURCHIX, and the dog. Until Baby became a mommy herself, delivering three kittens in the big closet in Shelby's and Stuart's bedroom. For weeks afterward, Shelby and the girls became live-in nannies. After a couple of months, it was time for the girls to live up to their promise to find other homes for the new litter; but by then they had become Tuffy, Peanut, and Pudge. Tuffy was adopted by a friend. At the insistence of the household women, led by Hope, Peanut and Pudge became permanent residents. Now the FOURCHIX had FIVE CATS, and Pudge became Hope's favorite. The two were almost inseparable.

HOPE HAD A WAY of becoming inseparable from things and people she loved. While her family grew into this knowledge, others would sometimes come to this understanding rather expediently. Such was the case for their new pastor.

Hope was only three years old when Ken Lyon joined Matthews United Methodist Church. The Stouts had been members for years. The church had a picnic to welcome the Reverend Lyon, and after lunch, he gathered the children for a story. It was a way to introduce himself and give the young ones a way to remember his name. He told the story of Daniel and the lions.

Whether it was the story itself, or the compelling way he told it–or the fact that lions are also cats, after all – an instant bond formed between Hope and her pastor. When Reverend

Lyon first took time out of the Sunday service for a children's message and called the kids around, she staked out a seat on the sanctuary steps *rightnexttohim*. It became Hope's special spot, and hers it was every single Sunday.

Faith was much more than a going-to-church thing for the Stouts, though to label them "religious" might miss the point. Faith was something they put into action in their own lives because it was who they were, not something to put on for show like a Sunday suit. To them, loving your neighbor was how you showed you loved God. It's how Stuart and Shelby were raised, and it was how they raised their girls. From the time they could carry a plate, they helped Shelby deliver meals to older people living alone, where the visiting and cheering up were as much what it was about as the food. Becoming teenagers meant going with Dad on REACH Week, a ministry where groups of young people from all over the country are brought to the smallest towns in rural America to refurbish homes for some of the poorest among us.

And there was Rainbow Express. It was a weeklong camp for special needs kids at the Stouts' church. There were teams of one youth leader and one camper buddy for each of the special kids. Hope had been a camper buddy since she was seven and it was one of her favorite weeks of the year. The leaders and buddies got as much out of Rainbow Express as the campers themselves, maybe more. They learned about putting others first; to see life through someone else's eyes and walk in their shoes. The campers may have had Down syndrome or autism or cystic fibrosis; but to the Stout girls, they simply had a few more challenges to overcome. Hope, in particular, hated the way the children were looked at differently by people. Or not looked at, at all, as she once told her mom.

"They're just normal kids!" she would tell Shelby. "They just want to be kids like everybody else."

HOPE WAS A NORMAL KID like every other in her love for TV shows like *SpongeBob SquarePants* and *Lizzy McGuire*, but she wanted to have her own show. Hope wanted to be like Oprah Winfrey. She pretended she was, hosting her own "Hope-rah Show." In a fifth grade report called, "My Life after Eleven Years," she drew a picture of her handprints in the cement at Grauman's Chinese Theatre in Hollywood. Hope was going to be a star! For Hope there was no small pretending, and no small dreaming. She played big and intended to live big. If ever there was a kid it seemed impossible cancer could attack, that kid was Hope Stout. Maybe that's why nobody thought all that much about the pain in her knee.

# CHAPTER 3

# A PAIN IN THE KNEE

SHE'D HAD IT for a couple of months, on and off, but does any parent of a 12-year-old figure a pain in the knee is going to turn out to be bone cancer? Headaches may ring the paranoia bell, but a sore knee? When it's the knee of a 12-year-old who's into tumbling, cheerleading, and basketball? Hope was always a little banged up. If it wasn't from diving after a basketball or dropping to her knees anchoring the pyramid in a cheer or hitting the mat while tumbling, it might have been playing football or tubing on the lake. It could have been anything, including that four-inch growth spurt triggering growing pains just as the other Stout girls had growing pains around that same age. For Austin and Holly those pains mostly served to engender sympathy, leg rubs, and girl talk with Mom, which is precisely what they did for Hope.

Besides, when the soreness didn't go away, Shelby had taken Hope to see the family pediatrician. He'd been the girls' doctor all their lives, and he didn't feel or see anything in the knee bone or ligaments that suggested anything serious. He suspected a strain from Hope's athletic pursuits and recommended an elastic brace and taking it a little easier for a while. He had put Hope through a demanding checkup, pushing and poking deep into Hope's knee before and after having her do rigorous stretches and deep knee bends. About the only thing he didn't do was take an x-ray.

That was mid-May 2003. The doctor did add that if the pain persisted after a couple weeks of wearing the brace and being more careful, Hope should see an orthopedist. By the middle of June, the knee was still hurting, so Shelby made the appointment. Even going this next step didn't seem like any big deal. Shelby had forgotten to even mention it to Stuart until he noticed Hope limping on her way back to the car after a family dinner out on Saturday, June 21.

"Shelby, she's really limping."

"Yeah, she told me a couple of days ago that her leg was really hurting, so I called the pediatrician. They made an appointment for her on Monday with an orthopedist."

It was the night before Stuart and Holly were leaving for REACH week, which this year would find them fixing up homes in Oliver Springs, Tennessee, about a five-hour drive from Charlotte. Stuart made a point of going in to see Hope as she headed for bed. He kissed her goodnight, flicked off the light, and was on his way out the door when she said, "Dad, my knee is really hurting."

"I saw you limping tonight after dinner. Lemme take a look."

As Stuart turned the light back on, Hope threw off the sheets, and he saw just how swollen his daughter's knee really was. It was huge. He reached out and applied a gentle touch. Hope's reflexes snapped a lightning-quick retreat.

"OW!"

Stuart caught his own startled recoil and somehow produced a calm, controlled reply.

"Ahhh, yeah. You're swollen there all right, kiddo, but you'll be fine once you see the doctor."

With a father's comforting hand on a daughter's red head and another kiss on her cheek, Stuart stuffed his sudden concern and walked out of Hope's bedroom to his own.

THE NEXT MORNING Stuart and Holly made the drive west through the Blue Ridge Mountains into Tennessee to Oliver Springs, a tiny town of 3,300 people, where REACH week was commencing. Sunday became Monday, and Stuart's efforts to block from his mind Hope's visit to the orthopedist that morning finally succeeded thanks to the hands-on instruction required to show a REACH girl how to remove the rotted old flooring in a bathroom they were refurbishing. He was actually *BEEP-BEEP* startled when his phone gleefully beeped just before noon that he had received a voice mail, but how *BEEP-BEEP* does a cell phone manage to get a signal to be able to tell you that you have a *BEEP-BEEP* voice mail when it doesn't get enough signal there in the Tennessee hills to get the *BEEP-BEEP* call in the first place? "ALL RIGHT!" Stuart barked at the phone. He left the house to call his voice mail. He was walking calmly, but his mind was racing.

When you've been married 24 years, your stomach can hear the first of your wife's words to make it through the broken signal before they even register in your brain.

"*Possible tumor…*

"*Biopsy Friday…*

"*Very scared…*

"*Please call…*"

Fear like he had never known invaded Stuart's consciousness. Minutes earlier and 300 miles away, the same fear had invaded Shelby. It stole his breath and buckled his knees, leaving him to stagger a few steps to sit on a wood pile just as it had left Shelby staggering breathlessly to a chair. Stuart hopped in a van and drove a half-mile from the work site to where he could get signal enough to talk with Shelby.

She told him the orthopedist had done x-rays and had found something. Maybe an infection. Possibly a tumor. In any case, he found a suspicious "something" that caused him to want a biopsy, and the soonest it could happen was Friday. Shelby got a call in to Pastor Lyon before Stuart phoned, and Stuart had been praying as he was driving. As they spoke, they began to calm each other. They drew on their deep faith to overcome a parent's deepest fear. They told each other all the right things, all the other things it could be, the suspicious something on the x-ray.

Stuart wanted to come home right then, but Shelby said no, because there was nothing anybody could do before the test Friday. Hope issued the ultimate verdict: "That's crazy, Dad. Stay up there with Holly. Me and Mom and Austin can handle this."

Stuart stayed, but only after winning agreement that he would return home a day early so that he and Shelby could take Hope to the hospital together. There, in a private waiting room on the fifth floor of Carolinas Medical Center, on Friday, June 27 – after four days that passed like a kidney stone – Stuart, Shelby, and Austin stood surrounded by family and Pastor Lyon as Dr. Jeffrey Kneisl, the surgeon who performed the biopsy on Hope only an hour earlier, entered, leaned back against a desk, took a deep breath, and exhaled.

"I'm afraid the news is not good."

OSTEOSARCOMA. A form of bone cancer, Kneisl explained. As if that most petrifying of words – cancer – wasn't "not good" news enough, the words that followed were horrific: *aggressive... spread... other leg... hip... back... lungs.*

The Stouts were still reeling from the shocking biopsy results when they were visited minutes later by Dr. Daniel McMahon, who was about to become their daughter's pediatric oncologist. (Who ever imagines their daughter will one day *have* a pediatric oncologist?) His words were like heat-seeking missiles that went straight for their hearts: *sorry... bad... rare... advanced.* He also borrowed from Dr. Kneisl: *other leg... hip... back... lungs.* So they *did* hear Kneisl say *lungs.* Holy God.

There was more. McMahon plowed ahead.

"Typically, with this type of cancer, we use traditional chemotherapeutic agents. However, in Hope's case..."

All eyes locked on the doctor, "Well..." as he looked straight at Stuart and Shelby, "with the level of Hope's disease, some parents would opt to do nothing; to not subject their child to chemotherapy, given the level of the disease. To... let nature take its course. I am not saying to do that, but..."

There it was. In less than an hour, a week's worth of Stuart and Shelby's uncontrollable leaps into dire scenarios and shuddering possibilities had come true. Their powerful prayers and pleas, along with those of an exponentially expanding chain of family and friends, had been overruled by reality. Cancer had indeed attacked the girl it would have seemed foolish to mess with. And as if the disease somehow knew there could be only one strategy that would give it a chance of winning, it had launched a diabolically clever attack, using Hope's own strength against her – her vitality. Hope's athleticism is where the cancer struck. It snuck in through her knee, one of the most-flexed joints in any active life, and even more so that of a kid hurtling her way through a life packed with cheerleading, tumbling, basketball, and tubing on the lake. Cancer crept in masquerading as a 5-foot-6-inch girl's growing pains. It camouflaged itself in her constant bumps and bruises and stitches and strains using the very nature of her own life as cover for its infiltration. Hope was doomed before she was even diagnosed.

"Well, we are *not* just giving up," Shelby shot back at Dr. McMahon, eyes filled with tears but a mother's instinct to fight for the life of her child having been fully triggered. "We are *not* just letting nature take its course. Hope will beat this thing. You just tell us what you recommend, and we'll do it."

The first thing they had to do was tell Hope, but they couldn't until the next morning. She was barely awake more than a couple of minutes at a time the rest of Friday, sleeping off the anesthesia and the effects of the surgery. When she finally woke up, Stuart and Shelby told her what the doctors had told them. She sat up in the bed with her head drawn down. She said very little. She didn't cry. Dr. McMahon soon arrived and introduced himself. He told Hope that he was going to help her get better.

"Do you have any questions for me?" he asked Hope.

More quiet.

She looked up.

"Will I lose my hair?"

# CHAPTER 4

# CARDIAC CATS

THE MONDAY AFTER THE WIN over Jacksonville, the Carolinas were electrified by the wild start to the Panthers' season, and the team basked in the buzz. For about three minutes. That's how long it took John Fox to bring their focus to the stark reality that lay ahead on Sunday: the reigning Super Bowl Champion Tampa Bay Buccaneers on their turf – the always-rowdy Raymond James Stadium.

The Panthers rolled into Tampa nine-and-a-half-point underdogs. It was the Bucs home opener, which meant it was the official celebration of their Super Bowl victory. They charged onto the field under their new championship banners, hoisting the shiny silver Super Bowl trophy. Along with nearly 66,000 crazed fans, they reveled in the memory of their conclusive 48-21 defeat of the Oakland Raiders. This was all going on in front of the Carolina Panthers and their new starting quarterback, Jake Delhomme.

The Bucs and their boisterous fans roared, but the Panthers did not cower, and an old-school NFL defensive battle developed. Through the game's first three grinding quarters, in sweltering 91-degree Florida sunshine, only twelve total points were scored. Four field goals. That all but one would come off the foot of Carolina kicker John Kasay, no one would have guessed.

The Panthers took their 9-3 lead into the fourth quarter and shut Tampa down the first three times they had the ball. With less than two minutes to go, the Panthers were forced to punt. The kick set the Bucs back on their own 18-yard line. This time, Tampa charged up the field like the Super Bowl champs they were, going 82 yards in eleven plays for a game-tying, fan-igniting touchdown just as the clock ran out.

The game was tied at nine. Regulation time was up. Having scored a touchdown though, the rules gave the Bucs the chance for the extra point that would give them a 10-9 win. Tampa fans, whose afternoon had started with a Super Bowl celebration, were now three hours more primed and ready to pop the cork on a win, as soon as the Bucs sealed their come-from-behind conquest with the one-point conversion kick, the surest thing in pro football. Usually.

As Martin Gramatica stepped into his kick, 335-pound Panther defensive tackle Kris Jenkins launched his 6-foot-4-inch frame over Tampa's offensive line, thrust his arms toward the sky, and blocked it. The crowd was stunned sober as the game went into overtime.

Now, the first team to score would win. The Panthers won the coin toss and got the ball first, but couldn't get close enough for a decent shot at a field goal. The Bucs were then similarly stifled. They punted to Steve Smith, who lit off on a blistering 52-yard return. You could feel the breath being squeezed out of the Buccaneer faithful as a couple of quick run plays put the Panthers on Tampa's 28. Bucs players on the field were as helpless as their fans in the stands as John Kasay booted his fourth field goal of the day, giving the Panthers a 12-9 overtime win.

Tampa fans didn't want to believe what their eyes had just seen. Carolina fans weren't entirely sure they could. Panther players themselves could barely believe it. The locker room was pandemonium, as though they had just won the Super Bowl. In beating the current champs, it felt almost like they had. Reporters caught up in the moment asked jubilant players, "How do you feel?" More than a few exclaimed on cue, "I'm going to Disney World!" In eight days these Cardiac Cats had staged an incredible double-come-from-behind victory to save opening day, then hit the road and toughed out an overtime win against the number one team in the league. When things settled down enough for him to speak, John Fox stood in the midst of his players and staff and summed it up.

"Men, that's the kind of game championship teams win."

TWO GAMES, TWO WILD WINS. Last seconds. Over-time. Blocked kicks. Clutch field goals. Big punt returns. Pressure passes. After spending the first half of the Jacksonville game in a coma, the Panthers played six straight quarters of inspired, explosive, heroic football. John Fox's desperate and bold move to put the offense in the hands of the desperate and bold Jake Delhomme had sparked the entire team. Every unit came through at one time or another to make those two heart-pounding wins happen.

There was nothing cardiac about the next game. "The I-85 Rivalry" it's called; the Carolina Panthers and the Atlanta Falcons. Panther Stadium and the Georgia Dome are each about three miles off Interstate 85 with only a three-and-a-half-hour ride down that highway separating them. In the third game of the season, the Panthers and their coaches finally had it all together and rolled over their rivals 23-3. The taste of their first decisive start-to-finish winning performance was sweet.

In another week, the Panthers would knock off Jake Delhomme's unrequited football love, the New Orleans

Saints, 19-13. It was an unspectacular game for Jake, but a spectacular game was not required. Running back Stephen Davis pounded out 159 yards and a touchdown, Rod Smart blew through the Saints for a 100-yard kickoff-return touchdown, and John Kasay pitched in a couple of field goals. While the game itself may not have been noteworthy, the win was. It gave the Panthers their first 4-0 start to the regular season – ever.

They had opened with three straight wins before, but always ran into a buzz saw for at least awhile after that. Just a year earlier, in 2002, the Panthers set off high hopes winning their first three in a row but were knocked off eight straight times after that. Now they were undefeated after four. Yet they had been expected to beat the Saints, who only had one win, and Atlanta was on their way to a seven-game losing streak when the Panthers played them. The Carolina Panthers were 4-0, but were they for real?

THEY WERE NOT IN THE SAME CLASS as the Indianapolis Colts. True, the Colts hadn't yet figured out how to get past the first round of the playoffs, but they had at least *made* the playoffs three of the last four years. It had been seven years since the Panthers last made the playoffs – or even had a winning season.

The Colts were also undefeated as they welcomed Carolina to the RCA Dome. They were led by six-year veteran, future Hall of Fame quarterback, Peyton Manning; the Panthers, by a guy entering only his fourth game as a team's official starter. Manning had rung up an average of 32 points in each of his wins; Jake only 20.

Players, coaches, and fans all knew the Colts would be the Panthers' toughest test yet. They knew this game would reveal whether the Panthers might actually be on a fantastic journey, or were just riding a bubble before it burst. This game would clearly show whether John Fox's win-by-not-losing, use-the-running-game-to-drive-the-offense, and live-off-your-defense strategy had *game* enough to carry the Panthers over one of the league's powerhouses.

John Kasay kicked Carolina onto the scoreboard with a field goal, while the Panther defense kept the Colts scoreless in the first quarter. Peyton Manning is never kept down for long though, and only ninety seconds into the second quarter, he led an 81-yard touchdown drive to give Indianapolis the lead, 7-3. Manning would control play for all but two and a half minutes of the second quarter. The Colts would score twice more, but the Panther defense kept them out of the end zone both times, so those other two scores were field goals, not touchdowns. The Panthers stayed within ten at halftime, 13-3.

Panther defender Ricky Manning Junior opened the second half by intercepting a Peyton Manning pass on the Colts' own 28-yard line. On the very next play, Jake handed the ball to Stephen Davis, who bolted for a touchdown, and took the edge off the crowd. The Panther defense set the offense up again on the next series by forcing Indianapolis to punt. Jake and the Panthers then showed Manning and company some shock and awe: a 52-yard touchdown pass to Steve Smith that gave Carolina the lead and put Indianapolis fans firmly in their seats.

Into the fourth quarter, the Panther defense shut Manning and the Colts down again and again and again. Kasay kicked another field goal to push the Panthers' lead to 20-13, but 3:08 on the clock is too much time to leave Peyton Manning, even starting from his own 9-yard line. He methodically marched his Colts to a touchdown on nine straight passes, sending fans into orbit and the game into overtime.

Luck was a Panther that day. The overtime coin toss gave Carolina the ball first. The Panther running game was by now driving the offense too smoothly to be kept out of field goal range. John Kasay swiftly kicked the Indianapolis Colts off the undefeated list and left RCA Stadium as quiet as an Indiana cornfield in July.

Carolina had done it again. Another edge-of-your-seat, *can-you-believe-it?* win. The third of the young season pulled out in the final seconds or overtime. If the kid out of nowhere, Jake Delhomme, made John Fox look like a genius on opening day against Jacksonville, the entire team in game five against Indianapolis made him look ingenious. The Cardiac Cats were now 5-0 and heading home to take on the Tennessee Titans the next Sunday, October 19.

On the field before the game would be a 12-year-old girl in a fiery red wig.

# CHAPTER 5

# BEACH WEEK

DESPITE THE URGENCY to retaliate against newly diagnosed cancer, treatment can't move forward until it can move forward. So after hearing more horrible truth than the Stouts could comprehend the Friday they got the news about Hope, what Dr. McMahon said to Stuart and Shelby that Saturday morning after meeting with Hope seemed downright bizarre.

"Have you got any plans for the Fourth of July?"

"Huh?"

*"Have you got any plans for the Fourth of July?"*

"We usually go to the beach. We had rented a cottage, but then…"

"By all means, go!"

"What?"

"Hope can leave as soon as her discharge papers come down. It'll take us about a week to get things squared away here anyway."

They had to schedule surgery to implant a catheter in Hope's chest that would be used for her chemo. Plus, there were details of tests to review and other preparations and plans to make. Even moving things along as rapidly as possible, McMahon said there was no reason for the Stouts not to make their annual Fourth of July family trek to Holden

Beach. They couldn't believe it. What they had just heard was truly not believable given what they'd heard just a day before. They told Hope.

"LET'S GET OUT OF HERE!"

Within thirty minutes they were on their way back to the house with Hope, and then welcoming Holly as she arrived with the rest of the group from REACH camp. They spent Saturday night at home and on Sunday morning, left for a week at the beach that they thought had vaporized with the news of two days earlier.

FAITH IS THE FOUNDATION of life for the Stouts, but as with many Carolina families, the beach is also a way of life. Summers are filled with vacation weeks or long weekends, especially holidays, spent at ancestral homes passed on through generations or at cottages rented for a week or a season at a time. Relatives and friends flee the stifling inland heat for the cool Atlantic breeze, the surf and sand, and the sunrises and sunsets of the Carolina coast. The center of the Stouts' summer universe was Holden Beach, a quiet seaside town of a few hundred people about halfway between touristy Carolina Beach and the perpetual partying of Myrtle. That was where their extended family gathered every Fourth of July.

This particular beach week was a gift they couldn't have imagined 48 hours earlier. Priceless memories were painting themselves on canvasses in their minds. Sunny days and starry nights were filled with beach food and beverages, rounds of golf, and chilling by the shore. There was escape TV to watch, family games to play, and lots of plain old vacation-vegging around the cottage. With its sprawling, screened-in front porch and seven rocking chairs, it served up sweeping views of the Intracoastal Waterway as far as the eye could see.

Gina Wheeling was there with Hope for much of the week. They were together at Holden often because Gina's grandparents lived there. One afternoon, the two girls and Stuart took a two-hour ocean voyage aboard a waterway neighbor's 42-foot cruiser. The girls were in full British accent as luxuriating royalty, waving the princess wave to commoners passing by on lesser vessels. Grand experiences weren't needed to have fun, though. Hope, her sisters, and Gina went with Shelby and Gina's mom on a "Ladies' Day Out" excursion to the mall on another day in nearby Wilmington. It's debatable whether there was more shopping or laughing.

It was an idyllic time, but a surreal one. The Stouts had just been through the most horrifying few days of their lives, and Hope's ultimate clash with cancer lay ahead. Yet there they were, living these dreamy days at the beach. As the days passed and that menacing future drew near, as Friday arrived bringing the traditional Fourth of July cookout, and as that last afternoon at the beach faded into their final night and the fireworks over the waterway – Hope was getting scared. They were all getting scared, and they began to dread going home.

It's never much fun, the drive back from the beach. This time getting back to Charlotte meant finally having to face the new fact of their lives: the baby of their family, Hope, the irrepressible redhead, had cancer. Deadly serious cancer. Not that every cancer isn't serious, but *bone cancer*. Cancer in a place people are afraid of other cancers spreading to; Hope's cancer started there. *Osteosarcoma*. What a hideous word. Fast-moving and aggressive. It had already proven its aggressiveness by stealing out from her knee, before they even knew it was there, to Hope's other leg, hip, back, and lungs. The girl who never did anything in a small way didn't get cancer in a small way, either.

Unpacking from Fourth of July on Saturday segued into packing for the hospital on Sunday. It was now time for Hope's first round of chemotherapy. The joy of beach week was never in the rearview mirror so fast.

# CHAPTER 6

# ACTION!

THIS WOULDN'T SEEM POSSIBLE, but the start of Hope's chemotherapy took them by surprise.

Shelby slept in the recliner in Hope's hospital room that Sunday night, and Stuart stayed home with the other girls. The Sunday night check-in was only so Hope would be there first thing in the morning, which is when the secret directors in hospitals always seem to shout, "Action!"

Into action everyone snapped. They all hit their marks and rolled Hope into surgery to implant the Hickman catheter at precisely 9:00 a.m. Monday, just after Stuart and Holly arrived. A few hours later, Hope was out of surgery and recovering from the anesthesia, and all were settling in for a day and night of watching TV and killing time until Tuesday morning. That's when the big moment would arrive. The overture would play, the secret director would again shout, "Action!" the curtain would rise, and Act One-Scene One of Hope's chemotherapy would finally begin.

Except there was no overture, no curtain rising. They heard no one shout, "Action!" Stuart had stopped at Wendy's for dinner that evening. They were eating and watching TV when yet another nurse walked in, as nurses endlessly do, to check yet another something *on* Hope or do yet another something *to* Hope.

This nurse wheeled an IV pole up next to the bed. Hanging on its hook was a clear plastic bag filled with some dark yellow fluid, and she was…

"What's that?" Hope asked.

…attaching the connector on the end of the plastic tubing of the IV to the port of Hope's catheter which protruded near her…

"This is cisplatin, the first of your treatments."

…collarbone, and with a touch of a button on the digital flow control, the mysterious yellow fluid began dripping into the tube, and the nurse was propping Hope up a bit on the pillow, and…

"I thought this was supposed to start tomorrow?" Shelby asked.

…stepping back to assess the scene before…

"Well, we generally start the treatment as soon as we can."

…leaving.

They stood speechless, looking at Hope. Watching. The drops fell into the tube and formed a steady trickle toward her chest. Wondering. As they were finishing off the bag of burgers, the chemotherapy and Hope's actual battle against her cancer had unceremoniously begun.

Eventually, Stuart asked Hope, "Do you feel any different?"

"Nope. Don't feel anything. Am I supposed to?"

"Apparently not," Shelby said.

By morning that would change. That night was the last of Hope not "feeling different" for a long, long time.

WE TEND TO THINK of chemotherapy as a chemical of some kind, given to somebody with cancer, and it goes off and fights the disease. Along the way, the chemical – the drug itself – makes the patient sick. Not exactly.

First round chemotherapy drugs typically don't know cancer from a pimple and go about killing the mutant cells by trying to kill all the cells in the body. The chemicals are trying to kill the cancer by almost, but not quite, killing the patient. The nausea and fevers and the rest are the body's attempt to fight for its life against chemicals trying to kill it in order to save it. In Vietnam's paradoxical parlance, chemotherapy is like *almost* destroying the village to save the village.

Cisplatin is an intense chemical. It is made from platinum, hence the cis-*platin*. It is a heavy metal and comes with strong warnings about headaches, seizures, diarrhea *and* constipation, numbness and tingling in the hands and feet, possible vision loss, possible hearing loss, kidney damage, mouth sores, vomiting, decreased white and red blood cell and platelet counts – and of course, the hair loss Hope feared.

Along with the cisplatin, they started her on Herceptin. This is actually a protein that tries to stop the growth of cancer cells by attaching itself to them and blocking their reproduction. It also seems to spark certain other cells that attack the cancer. Herceptin is only used in patients who test positive for a certain type of protein. It is most commonly used to treat breast cancer. Hope didn't have breast cancer, but she had tested positive for that same protein, so Dr. McMahon decided to give Herceptin a shot, too. A double-barreled blast at the cancer was encouraging. But Herceptin comes with its own long list of side effects, including stomach pain, diarrhea, severe nausea and vomiting, fevers and chills, headaches and dizziness, trouble sleeping, and weakening of the body's immune system.

So the skinny 12-year-old was having pumped into her body not one, but two furiously powerful cancer-fighting drugs, each with its own potentially raging side effects. And they were working. Whether they were working on stopping the cancer wouldn't be known for quite a while, but the drugs were working precisely as advertised in the side effects department. There were days and nights of violent vomiting and horrible diarrhea, of scorching fevers and drenching sweats and icy chills, and of every inch of Hope's body feeling pierced with pain. She wouldn't be well enough to leave the hospital until the end of that first long week, and even then, she kept getting sick at home. It would be weeks before she would come close to feeling normal. Just in time for the methotrexate.

This is a curious drug. It is an antimetabolite, which means it interferes with the metabolism of cells, inhibiting their reproduction. The curiosity is in the bizarre range of conditions it's used to treat. Injected or IV dripped into patients in high doses, methotrexate is deployed to fight cancer. In far lower doses, it is prescribed orally to treat psoriasis.

Methotrexate's antimetabolic action attacks all fast-growing cells, but somehow strikes the cancer cells quicker. The idea is to pump a patient up with enough of the drug to put the fast-growing cells on death row, then rapidly reverse course with a flood of IVs. The fluids, and the endless pit stops that come with them, are supposed to flush the system in time to give the *good* fast-growing cells a reprieve, while the *bad* fast growing cells have hopefully received a fatal dose of the mysterious metho. It is a chemical dance of life and death.

It typically takes three, maybe four days for enough methotrexate to be flushed before a patient can go home. Hope locked onto this estimate as a plan, so when it dragged on longer before the metho levels dropped enough for her to leave, it drove her crazy. As methotrexate round one pushed into its fifth and sixth days, Hope was now into her fifth and sixth week of being just plain sick. She understood that they were now actively fighting her cancer. Still, the fact remained, she felt far sicker since they had started trying to cure her cancer than when she was simply dealing with the knee pain. It wasn't just the chemo's relentless pounding on her body; the process was grinding on her mind and spirit. For a girl who practically lived outside having fun and getting into good, clean trouble, a summer of hospital stays and days and weeks in bed or on the couch was sheer torture.

Ravaged by what she was helplessly watching her daughter go through, Shelby had escaped to the hospital chapel one day. She collapsed to her knees as her numbed body couldn't stand it any longer. Alone in the small sanctuary, she poured herself out in a rush of prayerful anger.

"Why would you do this? We have prayer chains going all over the world, and we are not seeing any good results!"

As she opened her eyes, her gaze fixed onto a stained glass window immediately to her right. Shelby had prayed in the chapel before, but had never noticed it. It depicted a girl about Hope's age and height. She had injured legs and was on crutches – and she had bright-red hair.

The girl was standing next to the "Beloved Physician" as the caption on the scene described Him. She was being healed.

The pane was titled "The Hope Window."

# CHAPTER 7

# PLUNDERING VILLAIN

SOON IT WAS PUSHING mid-August. Beyond the frustration of being cooped up while her friends lived the lives 12-year-olds are supposed to be living, it was now back-to-school time. When you're a girl going into seventh grade, on the football cheerleading squad, and a star basketball player, you can't wait to go back. But Hope wouldn't be going back to school. Hope would be going back to the hospital. For chemo round three, metho round two.

The second round of methotrexate was pretty much the same as the first: pump her with enough to almost kill her, and then flush her like a rusty fire hydrant. After Hope got out of the hospital this time though, she started to feel like herself faster. Only two days after discharge, she was able to take a day trip with Shelby to Raleigh to help put more girlie touches on the room Stuart had moved Austin into at North Carolina State.

It was a day of dorm room decorating and campus cruising, and it was encouraging that Hope seemed to be doing so well. More encouraging, oddly, was her rapidly swelling knee. Stuart and Shelby were at first concerned about the way the knee was ballooning, becoming almost bone-hard and getting less and less moveable. McMahon explained that this sometimes happens as chemotherapy is killing the cancer cells. *Killing the cancer cells*? Words don't get any more encouraging than that.

Maybe they do. On Thursday, August 28, Dr. McMahon told them the best thing they'd heard since he had told them to head to the beach for the Fourth of July. He told them to head to the beach for Labor Day. It was marvelously uplifting news, which made the warmth Shelby felt as her hand brushed Hope's face the next morning all the more disheartening.

Everyone knew in a silent second what a fever meant. Hope tried valiantly to chase it away with bright smiles and upbeat declarations. Her blankets pulled way up, that's what made her warm, or the kittens piled on the bed. The thermometer was heartless. It proved again and again, as Hope demanded do-overs, a fever had snuck in overnight and stolen their beach trip away.

Five days back in the hospital. It wasn't all that scorching a fever, pushing 101 degrees, but it was serious. And it was completely unacceptable for a cancer patient going through chemo, so it demanded in-hospital infection fighting. It was a maddening, in-your-face reminder – as if they needed a reminder – that Hope's life, all of their lives, were not in their control. A plundering villain was on the loose. A very real, yet unseen outlaw they could never confront face-to-face, the way crime victims and their families are compelled to fill courtrooms to look a criminal in the eye. They were left to rage torridly, but almost theoretically, against this would-be killer of their little girl, and she was left increasingly in tears over the life it was thieving from her.

HOPE CERTAINLY KNEW she had cancer and could die, but death to a 12-year-old is an abstraction of the future. When she was diagnosed, her first question had been about losing her hair. All the sinister uncertainties of cancer and its too-often ultimate outcome, yet what a middle-school girl comprehends quickest is how she'll look. When the day of hair reckoning finally did come – a clump of her red locks suddenly dangling precariously off the side of her head one morning at breakfast – Hope had Emily help her brush it all out in favor of the wig that had been made for her. She didn't want to go through several awkward days of transition. Seeing the drastic change in Hope right before their eyes, what was happening to her, suddenly became real for both girls. Tears fell. Four streams. As Shelby picked up the piles of hair and placed them in a plastic bag, two more rivers flowed.

Death can be almost hypothetical to a child, but being cooped up in a hospital room day after excruciating day, having a gloriously imagined weekend at the beach given but then abruptly taken away, is all very real. She watched as summer flew by outside the window while her days were spent inside on the couch throwing up. Day after day it went on, life inexorably passing Hope by. Summer life passing by gave way to back-to-school life passing by, which meant seventh grade life beginning to pass by. All to an ever-more discouraging effect. Hope was rapidly plunging into despair. In her desperation, she would finally ask the question that in her hopefulness she had not.

It was Sunday, September 7. Gray, drizzling, and thickly-warm in Charlotte, and the Stout home was as dismal as the day. Stuart and Holly had gone to the Carolina Panthers' 2003 season opener against the Jacksonville Jaguars. Another day, Hope would have watched the game on TV. The mother-daughter alone time gave her the chance to become, for a moment, the child she couldn't be while fighting cancer.

Shelby climbed in bed with her as Hope asked for the first time, "Why me, Mom?"

Cuddled with her mother she pleaded, "Why is God doing this to me? Why can't I just be a normal kid?"

How does a mother answer the heart-wrenching questions of a frightened child that no words can possibly answer? With the loud, unspoken love of a hug. Shelby lay in bed with Hope as she had when she was a baby, holding her closely, endlessly. While the mother holds the baby to calm the crying, Shelby held Hope to let her cry. Hope needed to. Shelby knew the only end to her baby's crying would be depletion.

"I would trade places with you in a second if I could," Shelby wished in a whisper, as quiet replaced the crying.

"I would never, ever let anyone take this journey for me, Mom." Hope smiled, the comforted turning comforter, their hug still engaged, but the squeeze now transmitting from daughter to mother.

"No matter how bad it is."

A FEW WEEKS LATER, methotrexate round three came dressed as methotrexate round two just as round two had come dressed as round one. Familiarity did breed contempt. Hope hated the treatments, and knowing precisely the pumping and flushing and side effects that were coming when the metho started flowing, only made the experience more wretched.

If there was one thing carrying Hope and the whole family through this contemptible third round of metho, fourth round of chemo, it was knowing that they were nearing a milestone. Dr. McMahon had planned successive waves of chemotherapy – an initial "air war" of cisplatin and Herceptin followed by a "ground war" of several rounds of methotrexate – then a comprehensive review of the results. A complete re-diagnosis would determine precisely where they stood before launching one more blast of cisplatin and a final round of metho. They were all anxious, but hopeful, for the results. The big meeting set for September 24 was now only days away. Even as Hope was experiencing the predictable hell of more methotrexate, she was going optimistically through an exhaustive series of tests in preparation for the medical team's review.

She had three MRIs, a chest x-ray, an echocardiogram, a bone scan, an audiology test (checking for possible chemo-caused hearing loss), and seemingly endless blood work. A PET scan had been done along with other tests a few days earlier. Her methotrexate reading finally fell to the "you-can-get-the-heck-out-of-here" level Saturday morning, September 20, and by noon, Hope and her family had done exactly that.

She had waged a heck of a battle, and Holly, Austin, Stuart, and Shelby had battled right alongside her. They fought *with* her. Stood by her. Kept her close to them. Hope's cancer had struck the whole Stout family.

They had four days to pass before The Big Meeting.

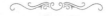

# CHAPTER 8

# A FAMILY THING

SAM MILLS IS A BIG PART of Carolina Panther history. He was on the original 1995 team, signing with the fledgling franchise after several years as a New Orleans Saint. Mills was a crunching linebacker, but he was 36 years old, and the crunching catches up with you. How many seasons he had left nobody knew, but the Panthers needed to pepper their brand-spanking-new roster with some key veterans, and Mills was just the guy on defense. He'd been a standout for the Saints, making the Pro Bowl team four times. Perhaps most important to the young Panther group, he was a leader. Not a running-at-the-mouth kind of leader, but a leader by example. A leader on the field. A leader in the locker room. Sam Mills was a leader of men because he was a man men wanted to follow.

As the Panthers came to life and fans packed the stands, Number 51 was always there. Though he was one of the oldest guys on the team, Sam Mills was the only Panther to start every game those initial three seasons.

He was entering the twilight of his career when he joined the Panthers, but he was rejuvenated in Charlotte. He even made the Pro Bowl again at age 37. He retired after the '97 season and a year later, rejoined the Panthers as linebacker coach, an inspired choice by the team, and a great decision by Sam. He was born for the job.

One of Sam's linebackers heading into 2003 was Mark Fields. Fields was an eight-year veteran the Panthers had grabbed the year before as John Fox set out to rebuild the team on the shoulders of the defense. He'd been a first-round pick by the New Orleans Saints in the 1995 draft and made the Pro Bowl in 2000. At 6-feet-2, 244 pounds and lightning fast, Mark Fields was made to order for the aggressive John Fox-Sam Mills approach to defense. He became a monster his first season with the Panthers. Number 58 led the team with 127 tackles, including fifteen in one game against the Pittsburgh Steelers. He sacked quarterbacks and caused fumbles. His stellar play-making made Mark Fields a fan favorite after only one season.

When training camp had opened for the 2003 season, the Panthers already looked good. A vibe was growing. There was serious buzz building about the defense. So when Mark Fields was diagnosed with Hodgkin's disease, it was a staggering kick in the players' guts. Two weeks later, when they learned that doctors had found cancer in Sam Mills' intestine, the team was devastated.

FOOTBALL PLAYERS BECOME like blood brothers. Relationships forged among members of a team are intimate and intense. For seven months they live and breathe and eat and travel and practice and plan and study and get hurt and get sick and get better and kill time together; they play practical jokes on each other; they win and lose together. There is the actual work of the job itself, the *combat* of the sport: hand-to-hand against each other in practice, hand-in-hand with each other in games. There is much blood and more sweat. They try to hide the tears. The guys are not all best friends; sometimes far from it. Yet if they are to succeed, the players will become part of each other. They will come to depend on each other physically, mentally, emotionally, and spiritually. They will remain individuals, but will also become as one. Sam's and Mark's cancer struck the whole Panther team.

Professional athletes are playing a sport, a game, a game they've been playing non-stop since they were kids. They haven't had to leave childhood things behind and become accountants or car salesmen or construction workers. While it's a tough road in its own ways, being a pro athlete can also be as idyllic as impudent youth, leaving adult realities *out there* somewhere. Cancer brought real life to the Panthers. Life's ultimate reality – death – was lurking right there in the locker room, inside Sam and Mark.

Overnight, Fields and Mills had a whole new fight to fight, and it wasn't for a division title or championship ring. Football games sometimes take on life and death dimensions; seasons, apocalyptic proportions. Through Sam and Mark, the Panthers were awakened to the meaninglessness of football, yet it was then that football took on a deeper meaning.

No one can fight anyone else's cancer battle for them. What can be done is to fight *with* them. Stand by them. Keep close to them. Keep them close to you. Football and the 2003 season became the way the Carolina Panthers could fight with Mark Fields and Sam Mills.

THE IDEA FOR THE T-SHIRTS came from equipment manager Jackie Miles, and the team jumped on it. Several players had been talking about doing something for Sam and Mark, and Miles had the brainstorm. White sleeveless tees with bold, black, four-inch numbers "58" and "51" printed on the chest, right over the heart, underneath a small snarling panther. Players wore them under their jerseys and pads on game days. The shirts were meant as a simple signal to Sam and Mark that they were on the field with their brothers every week and their brothers, in turn, were always with them. They came to mean so much more.

Picture the locker room. In the swirling mass of people, equipment, and activity that is 53 players and dozens of coaches and staffers readying for a professional football game, there was one dominating sight – those T-shirts. Everywhere were the numbers 58 and 51. Sam Mills and Mark Fields were pervasive in the locker room. Each shirt was that player's confirmation to himself and declaration to others that Sam and Mark were with him that day. No one was told to wear them, but everyone did. The shirts became the symbol of the Panthers' season, the meaning of their performance as players that went beyond football.

On the field and on the sidelines, every player became 58 and 51, because the numbers could be seen under their jerseys. They could be seen through many of the coaches' shirts too, including John Fox's. Not at all ironically, 58 and 51 could often be seen even clearer as each game wore on. As sweat streamed out of players' bodies and soaked their jerseys, those two numbers became like billboards. As each Sunday's going got tougher, the shirts became in-their-face reminders to the Panthers of their commitment to Sam and Mark – and to each other. If Mark and Sam could find the strength to keep pounding in their fight against cancer, then certainly the players could find the strength to keep pounding against Jacksonville, Tampa, or Indianapolis. And if Sam and Mark were inspiring the Panthers to keep pounding, then maybe the Panthers could inspire Sam and Mark to keep pounding.

NFL brass saw 58 and 51 through the Panthers' jerseys too, and they didn't like it. They sent word to Charlotte that they understood how the players and coaches felt but ordered them to drop the shirts. They interfered with the official "look" of the league-approved uniforms.

No way. The guys weren't going to give up the shirts. Jackie Miles, John Fox, and General Manager Marty Hurney agreed. They fought the league for Sam and Mark and for the whole team, and the league fought back. The T-shirts stayed.

Fans could also see 58 and 51 under the jerseys and knew exactly what the shirts represented. They clamored to be a part. Deep emotional fandom is *the way* in the Carolinas. Think ACC basketball. Think Carolina, Duke, or Clemson. Think NASCAR. No baseball idol in New York or basketball star in Chicago or hockey great in Boston ever had fans more fevered than the diehards for Junior Johnson, Richard Petty, or Dale Earnhardt.

Maybe it's a Southern thing, a reflex not strictly of that long-ago war but of the pillaging of the South during reconstruction and the pillorying of Southerners since. The South's been "doing it again" for a long time, to quote Charlie Daniels. Southerners wear their hearts on their sleeves, pull together and push hard for their own because nobody else does.

Maybe it's a "Mayberry" thing. Sheriff Andy Taylor's North Carolina hometown was fictional, but Andy Griffith's actual home, Mount Airy, is quite real, and it's just up the highway from Charlotte. They're not all that different, the two towns. Charlotte just happens to have grown to more than two million people, and there's probably not even six degrees of separation between most of them and the sheriff or the mayor – or the local sports star. Mayberry's iconic glimpse into life lived where lives really matter is truth through a lens refracted more than it is fiction fabricated.

To some extent it's a Jerry Richardson thing. The Panthers had become the first NFL team in the 650 miles between Atlanta and Washington, D.C., and rapidly developed a tight bond with their fans owing in no small part to decisions he made. He paid for the stadium in Charlotte by selling permanent seat licenses and putting the names of the 43,000 fans who bought them in stone out in front. He instantly made friends by the hundreds of thousands in South Carolina, as well as North, by setting up training camp at Wofford College in Spartanburg, his alma mater, and playing the inaugural season in Memorial Stadium at Clemson University while the new stadium was being built.

Southern thing, Mayberry thing, Jerry Richardson thing – bottom line, it had become a family thing. When there's a celebration, everyone celebrates; when there's a hurt, everyone hurts. In less than ten years a relationship had been woven between the Carolina Panthers and their fans such that when real life invaded football life and two Panthers were attacked by cancer, everyone felt attacked. Everyone wanted to fight back.

After the overtime win in Tampa, the team announced that the 58-51 shirts, and towels with the same logo, would go on sale starting the next Sunday. The money would go to a "Drop the Hammer on Cancer" drive the Panthers had launched to raise money for research in honor of Sam and Mark. The team would also kick in $500 for every touchdown, quarterback sack, and field goal the rest of the season; auction off autographed jerseys and footballs; set up donation points outside the stadium on game days; and launch a website for online giving. Good old-fashioned checks could also be sent in.

And they were – checks sent in, cash and coins tossed in canisters, T-shirts and towels bought and worn and waved.

Fans began making supportive signs and bringing them to the stadium, holding them high for Mark and Sam, the team, and the TV cameras. Hope Stout spent two hours working on hers the Saturday before the undefeated Panthers would host Tennessee.

## CHAPTER 9

# BEYOND A REASONABLE DOUBT

"MR. STOUT, I want to talk with you about the test results on Hope."

Dr. McMahon had called Stuart's cell phone first thing the morning of September 24. That was not the plan.

Stuart, Shelby, and Hope were all supposed to meet the doctor later. They would get the rundown of all the test results, the complete re-diagnosis, to determine precisely where they stood before launching those final victorious rounds of chemo. They were all anxious. Stuart had wishfully planned a relaxing round of golf with friends for later that comfortable fall afternoon and had snuck into his office early to clear his desk and mind of work. When his cell phone rang and the caller ID displayed "Daniel McMahon," he knew there would be no golf.

"We have had some rather extraordinary changes."

The lowered, controlled, "professional-medical-doctor" tone of McMahon's voice told Stuart he did not mean "extraordinary" in a good way. Stuart tried to brace himself for what his gut already knew was coming. Those people who tell you life seems to freeze or move a frame at a time when something horrible is happening? They must be lying.

"We have reviewed the test results and…" McMahon jumped right in.

*Jesus, this wasn't even supposed to be…*

"…even though there was some initial reduction in the tumors, the cancer grew back once the chemo stopped and…"

*happening this way this morning. Stuart shouldn't even have been hearing the doctor's voice over the phone like this, but he was and the words…*

"…has in fact spread to other areas."

*kept coming like a runaway freight.*

"There is new cancer in her shoulder and other spots now on her lungs, and the growth is unlike anything I have ever seen. I'm very sorry to have to tell you this."

Stuart's heart was trying to punch its way out of his chest, and now – NOW – life seemed to switch into slow-mo, a pause button of some kind hit for a second that felt like forever. A tense silence hung over the call. McMahon knew to wait for Stuart to speak, which he finally did, intending to ask, *What happened? What changed? We thought we were making progress?*

What came out of Stuart's mouth instead was the question he had fought from the beginning to keep from asking. The question he now couldn't keep himself from asking because it was the only one that mattered.

"Doc, level with me. Is this a terminal situation?"

"Yes, Mr. Stout. I'm afraid it is."

Stuart may have choked hearing those words. He may have doubled over. It was all a blur. His phone had rung while he was having coffee with a co-worker, but he had walked into his own office to take the call. He now found himself slumped in his chair at his desk as McMahon spelled it out.

"The level of Hope's disease to start with was significant, but we have clear evidence now that in spite of the treatment, the disease has grown. That is the reason I called. I want to meet with you and Mrs. Stout, without Hope being present, to discuss this further. As you know, Hope is supposed to come in tomorrow to begin another round of chemotherapy and…

"Frankly…

"I am not sure it is worth putting her through it."

DR. MCMAHON SHOWED STUART the most recent PET scan and x-rays, placing them on his desk next to the ones taken in June. They were to steal your heart away.

"I don't need to see those," Shelby conceded.

Calming himself as best he could after McMahon's phone call, Stuart had gotten his wife out of work in a vague ruse about the doctor's office needing to move up the appointment, so he would pick her up and they would run over. Once in the car, Shelby caught on instantly that McMahon wanted to see her and Stuart without Hope. Stuart held back the facts that had already brought him literally to his knees, but Shelby knew. Mothers know. She pressed Stuart no further and rode to the hospital staring out her window, silent, but for the sounds of sorrow.

In the office, Shelby faced away from Dr. McMahon's desk and the telltale x-rays, holding herself in folded arms for comfort, and perhaps also, to keep herself from reflexively turning for a glimpse. If she had looked, she would have seen that Hope's right leg, from her knee up through her hip, was now covered with cancer. There was a large mass in her left leg, ominous heavy dots on her spine and lungs, and an already formidable tumor about the size of a baseball on her shoulder.

The evidence Stuart saw was overwhelming; far beyond a reasonable doubt. Try though he did – with all power of human will and a father's limitless urge to fight for his child's life – Stuart couldn't deny that it seemed impossible that all that cancer could be eliminated.

"There are other treatments," McMahon said. He spoke thoughtfully and chose his words carefully. "But they may jeopardize Hope's health. We have a chemo treatment called VP-16. It is very severe. I must tell you, it could cause her death in and of itself."

Then the doctor cleared his throat and pushed his glasses up squarely on his face.

"Frankly, a lot of people would do nothing at this point. With the level of her disease being what it is, many people would let nature take its course, to use a term I am not comfortable with."

*Again* he was talking about "letting nature take its course."

Shelby had finally had enough of reality's crippling cannon fire and shot back. Not at Daniel McMahon, but through him, at the cancer that was quite obviously on Sherman's March through her baby.

"Well, I can tell you one thing… we are NOT giving up! If there is a CHANCE this can cure her, we are going to try!"

Only Hope didn't want to try.

HOPE HAD BEEN THROUGH four rounds of chemo-therapy, brutal in every way you hear it can be. Exceptionally so, as this skinny young child had been pumped with adult-sized doses of some of the most powerful chemicals in an oncologist's arsenal. They had turned all their cancer-fighting fury loose from her insides out, attacking virtually every cell and function in her body, in the prospect they would beat her cancer into submission. For eighty days she had fought, beginning the night of July 7, when to everyone's surprise a nurse had strolled casually in with an IV and nonchalantly started the cisplatin flowing. Eighty days she battled bravely – an eternity in the life of a child – gamely facing unknowns that would leave adults quaking with fear, only rarely revealing the strains of the struggle in protest or tears. For eighty endless days she had done all she had been asked by the professionals and her parents in the name of saving her from the vicious assailant that was trying to kill her. But the re-assessment showed she was sicker on Wednesday, September 24, than the day her battle had begun. The cancer was winning.

Stuart and Shelby knew they had to tell Hope about the meeting with Dr. McMahon, and they knew they had to tell her the truth. She was watching TV in the playroom they had at the top of the stairs. Hope had taken to camping out up there when she wasn't in the hospital. There was a comfortable futon which, being lower to the ground than her bed, was much easier for Hope to get into and out of for all those trips to the bathroom. Stuart took a seat on the end as Shelby knelt right up to Hope and softly and tenderly told her the truth. The whole truth. About the cancer spreading, about the treatments so far just not working, and about the VP-16. Another chemo. A long-shot maybe and a tough treatment, maybe even tougher than the others, but a chance. A chance maybe it could stop the cancer. They would try it, Shelby assured Hope, because they were not giving up. They were going to keep on trying to kill the cancer. Her mom and dad and sisters and everybody loved her, Shelby said, and they were not going to give up this fight.

Hope wept.

She sat for a few moments, thinking.

Thinking *who knows what* a girl not yet thirteen would think while facing one of the most deadly of diseases when she had just braved nearly three grinding months of the most barbarous of treatments in a desperate struggle for a cure only to be told – no matter how softly and tenderly – no dice? All the tests and needles and chemicals, all the fevers and chills and headaches, all the savage relentless puking and peeing and… *all that* didn't work? Oh, but now there's another medicine, another chemical, another treatment, which might – *might* – make a difference? And, by the way, this one could be worse than everything she'd already gone *pointlessly* through?

At whatever thoughts she was thinking, Hope wept. As they kindled in her mind, she cried. As it all surged through her, she cried harder, inconsolably, until finally, as her mind raced and her thoughts boiled over, and she imagined going through it all again and it being even more horrible, Hope finally exploded.

"WHAT'S THE USE?" she screamed at no one in particular. "I don't want to go to the hospital again! *PLEASE* don't make me! Let me just stay here at home, *PLEASE?*"

She exploded, and they let her – Stuart, Shelby, and Holly, who was there now too. They let her, knowing she just had to. The things she'd been told, the facts she'd had to face, were as poisonous to her mind as the cisplatin, Herceptin, and methotrexate were to her body. In a similar way, they had to take their course and blast their way out of her, too. So they let her rant and rage, let her fling her crutches against a bathroom wall, let her go off and secretly fume some more. Gradually, they each wandered away giving Hope the space and solitude she needed.

When things had gotten quiet for a while – eerily, almost frighteningly quiet – they made their way back. They found Hope scrunched behind a nightstand in the farthest corner of her parents' bedroom, as hidden from the world and her nightmare as she could get. They sat with her, at first not speaking, simply being there. In her family's quiet presence, Hope's racing thoughts seemed to run their course. Her crying broke, with deeper breaths now coming in between sobs; sobs increasingly of resignation, of surrender. When the passing moments allowed loving words of understanding and encouragement to flow naturally and effortlessly and genuinely from her mom and dad and sister – and when all those cats Hope loved, who had been her constant companions on the home front of her battle, sprang all over her – Hope's sobs of surrender and resignation broke into sobbing laughter. And with a few more laughs and breaths deeper still, sobs of determination.

Before long, they were on their way to the hospital.

# CHAPTER 10

# HAIL MARY

VP-16 IS A HAIL MARY. To Catholics, the "Hail Mary" is the prayer of the desperate, and in football, it's the desperate pass the quarterback throws as the last seconds of a game are ticking away, his team about to lose. The ball is heaved long and high into the end zone, which is flooded with receivers, in the last-gasp hope that one of his guys will come down with it for a touchdown to save the day. This was where Hope now stood in her battle with cancer. This was the situation the Stouts faced. They were up against the wall with time running out, so call the Hail Mary play. Break out the VP-16. There are cases where different levels of the drug are used to treat other cancers - some testicular cancers, for example - as a regular course of treatment and not as the last-ditch effort. But VP-16 is generally known as a final shot at cancers that haven't been stopped by anything else.

Its real name is etoposide. Dr. McMahon had described it as a more intense chemo treatment. He told them it would take Hope's white blood cell count down to practically nothing and jeopardize her health. The warnings actually say:

"Severe lowering of blood counts may occur causing infection or bleeding – sometimes fatal."

"Nausea and vomiting may be 'quite severe,' and 'drug therapy' may be needed to control the sickness."

"It is rare, but it has 'been known to cause leukemia.'"

"Caution is advised when using etoposide in children because they may be more sensitive to allergic effects of the drug."

And this:

"Certain types of plastics such as IV bags have been known to crack or leak when undiluted etoposide is used."

Well, who *wouldn't* want their little girl pumped full of *that* stuff?

No one would want that, of course. Unless it was the only thing left to do. What must it feel like as parents to know that the only thing you can possibly do to try to save your precious daughter is to put her through that? But that was exactly where the Stouts were, and so less than 24 hours after getting the cataclysmic update from Dr. McMahon, they were all back in the hospital, with VP-16 dripping into the port in Hope's chest. The Hail Mary had been thrown.

There was one saving grace in this fifth and most ferocious round of chemotherapy. Hope was now being given substantial pain medication to help her cope with the cancer and the intense effects of the VP-16, and it was knocking her out. Though she was wrestling with the predicted side effects of the chemo, she would zone off to sleep quickly between bouts.

Everyone tried to make the best of it during Hope's hospital stays. A group that had become known as the Decorating Bandits – Holly and Austin, along with Stuart's cousin Wendy Reeder, who was like a sister to him – would land with posters and props and all kinds of fun stuff and create colorful themes in the hospital room. There had been a *SpongeBob SquarePants* cartoon theme and a Jimmy Buffet motif with palm trees and parrots; a frog theme (F.R.O.G.: Fully Rely On God), and a beach theme before the Labor Day trip that ultimately didn't happen. They would have movie parties or watch TV shows together. More than once, Holly and Austin smuggled up Hope's favorite cat, Pudge, in a duffle bag for a visit, which always brought laughs and guilty *SSSHHHs!* when they'd see doctors or nurses walk by, which of course, would set off more laughter.

The Sunday during Hope's VP-16 treatment was the third Sunday of the football season, and the Bandits had planned a Carolina Panthers party. It was an in-hospital tailgate complete with Kentucky Fried Chicken and Panther jerseys. Hope wore number 90 for Pro Bowl defensive end and former University of North Carolina star Julius Peppers. It was the day of the game against the Atlanta Falcons when the team was going to start selling the 58-51 T-shirts. Austin and Holly were going to the game and stopped by on their way. It was great fun as always, but this time the fun backfired. When four o'clock rolled around and Stuart flicked on the TV to watch the game, the sight of Panther Stadium filled with jubilant, carefree fans got to Hope.

The stadium, packed with 72,000 fans including her two sisters, was only three miles up the street. Yet all the color and excitement and life she saw on screen – which in years prior had included her – felt a million miles from what her life had become. She didn't blame her sisters for going. She didn't begrudge them personally. But *she* loved the Panthers, too. *She* loved to go to the games. Why couldn't *she*? Why did *she* have to have this cancer? Why couldn't she just be a normal kid? A kid like everybody else.

She bore the burden of her disease far better than most adults probably would, but this day, this time, it was just too much. They flicked off the TV.

HOPE WAS ABLE TO GO HOME on Tuesday, but the warnings about fever, low blood counts, and the risk of infection proved true on Friday. As they rushed back to the hospital, Hope was getting sicker by the minute. Dr. McMahon met them, and stayed cool as always, but didn't hide his concern when he saw Hope and quickly checked her vitals. Her fever was climbing, by then over 101, and her blood pressure was fading to a frightening 80 over 25. She was dehydrating. He ordered an IV, walked Stuart a few steps down the hall, and warned him that Hope could be going into shock. McMahon paged a pediatric intensive care doctor who took one look and ordered her into his unit.

As fast as Hope slipped into this spiral, she whirled right out of it once she was in the PIC-U and the fluids got flowing. After an hour, she was moved to a regular room in the oncology ward. Stuart stayed, insisting Shelby get a night of rest at home for a change. He was sitting in the recliner next to Hope's bed, doing paperwork late into the evening as she slept, when Dr. McMahon walked in. Odd, seeing the oncologist there at that time of night. Panic was Stuart's immediate reaction. He launched himself out of the recliner. McMahon waved Stuart to sit back down and pulled up a chair alongside.

Silently, soberly, he removed his ever-present glasses, rubbed the long day out of his eyes, and crossed his legs in a futile attempt to get comfortable. He exactingly returned the glasses to their home and breathed a deliberate breath.

"For a few minutes there, I thought we were going to lose her."

"DAD! WAKE UP! LOOK!"

It was Saturday morning, and Hope startled Stuart out of the sleep he had finally fallen into. She was sitting up in bed and turning to get out to go to the bathroom – *by herself*.

"Hang on, I'll help you!"

"No, I don't need any help – just watch!"

Hope flopped her legs over the side of the bed, grabbed one of her crutches from against the wall, and headed for the bathroom. She even put a little weight on her right leg for the first time in weeks.

This was stunning! What happened? When Stuart had dozed off the night before, Hope was in a deep sleep, recovering from an episode her doctor had made a point of telling him almost killed her. Now, he was seeing more life and spark in his little girl than he'd seen in, well, he couldn't even remember. Hope was beaming. She was able to lift the leg the cancer had first attacked – that was so swollen and had become so hardened and stiff – two feet off the bed. When McMahon came by to check on her a short time later, she was able to let him poke and prod the leg and knee which had become virtually untouchable.

"This is truly a good sign," McMahon said, a rare look of relief coming to the reserved physician's face. He said the VP-16 had obviously knocked back enough cancer cells to drive sudden, dramatic improvement. The drug is harsh, it is risky, but sometimes the Hail Mary pass is caught. That's why you take the shot.

There was a long road ahead. There would be more chemo. But the VP-16 that had hit Hope so hard, had hit her cancer equally so. She felt terrific in that way that when you've been sick for a long time and you've forgotten what feeling good feels like and you can't imagine you ever will again, but then all at once the fever or flu or whatever cracks that first bit, and you're not even close to being truly better but it's such a startling change to feel even a *smidge* of good again after the horrible you've been feeling, that you feel like you're feeling terrific even though you're actually still a long way from it – that's how Hope felt that morning. Her fever still hung on, though, and not wanting to risk another episode like the one that led to the close call less than 24 hours earlier, McMahon kept Hope in the hospital a few days more. But on Wednesday, she would go home.

HOME! For Hope and for everyone, getting out of the hospital, this time especially, seemed such a wonderful blessing. Over those final precautionary days in the hospital she strengthened steadily, and while taking it easy at home, got stronger still. By mid-October she was feeling and looking and getting around better than she had in months. Having spent so much time living in the cancer and the chemo and the confinement of bed – whether at home or the hospital – Hope would waste no time leaping back into her living-large ways. Who would have guessed? After the awful assessment September 24, the intimidating, rocket-sounding VP-16 had launched Hope into an orbit that would bring a brush with death one day, but only fourteen days later, the weekend of a lifetime.

Friday night, October 17: Football game – Weddington High School. It's where Hope would go in two years, like Austin and Holly before her. She'd been going to football games there with family and friends for years. Able to get out and about at last, Hope wasn't going to miss the Homecoming game. Wasn't going to miss Holly being crowned sophomore attendant. Wasn't going to miss those sweet, soft, chocolaty-glazed Krispy Kreme donuts they sold as a school fundraiser at every game.

Saturday, October 18: Boone – North Carolina Mountains. A funky college town about two hours away. Home to

Appalachian State University. It was peak weekend for fall color along the Blue Ridge Parkway as the leaves were turning from green to gold and blazing bronze, bright-red, rust and amber. But the Mast General Store on King Street downtown was all that mattered to Hope.

It's right out of a movie, but it's real. An old-time mercantile store with creaky wooden floors, heavy glass doors with big brass door knobs, cash registers with all those buttons to punch with black and white numerals that pop up. It's stocked full of outdoor clothes, camping supplies, and rocking chairs; housewares, bags of ground flour, jars of fresh honey – everything conceivable, including a gigantic treats emporium.

There is an ancient reach-in cooler with bottles of grape Nehi and orange Crush; actual glass bottles with actual crimped-on metal bottle caps that you open using the opener on the side of the cooler, where you angle the bottle in and push it down and *POP* the cap off. They have racks and racks of peanut brittle, salt water taffy, macaroons, and moon pies. And candy. Barrels of candy. Bulging barrels of every kind of candy imaginable.

Mary Janes, Red Hots, Good & Plenty, and Oh Henrys. Jawbreakers, Slo Pokes, Sugar Daddies, and Black Jack gum. Pixy Stix, Bulls Eyes, malted milk balls, and Fizzies. Root Beer Barrels, Licorice Laces, Skittles, and Snickers bars – and of course, Gummi Bears, Hope's favorite. It's sold the old-fashioned way: by the pound. Grab a basket, pile it high, plop it down on the scale on the oak and glass counter. And boy did she! And did her mom's and dad's eyes pop at the size of the mountain. And did they battle to hold back the tears as they watched their cancer-battling daughter be something she hadn't been for months – a 12-year-old kid.

Sunday, October 19: Panther Stadium – Charlotte. The undefeated Carolina Panthers versus the Tennessee Titans. Over 69,000 fans were in the stands.

Hope Stout was down on the field.

SHE WAS NO CASUAL PANTHER FAN, yet she hadn't been to a game all season. She was crazy-frustrated being stuck at home or in the hospital while her sisters or her dad, or anybody else for that matter, got to go. Feeling as good as she finally was, Hope was darn sure going to make this one. The Stouts had their own season tickets, but a police officer friend who handled stadium security on game days had gotten them Club seats – some of the best in the stadium – and also scored pre-game field passes. As if that wasn't enough, Hope had also gotten word that maybe there'd be a surprise before the game. There was no guarantee, but "maybe" has a way of opening a 12-year-old's eyes wide with anticipation.

With best friend Emily Rutherford by her side, Hope set off for the Panther game with her dad and mom. Stuart and Shelby had tried to keep Hope's expectations in check as best they could. They couldn't. Hope knew something big was going to happen. She just didn't know how big.

"How big" would turn out to be 6-feet-5-inches and 310 pounds. "How big" would stand even taller in football cleats and loom larger still in football pants with sewn-in thigh armor, massive shoulder and elbow pads, arm wraps, and gloved hands taped up till they looked like enormous mitten-clubs. "How big" would be wearing a bright-blue and black and silver Carolina Panther jersey with gigantic white numerals "6" and "5" and the name "DONNALLEY" stitched on it.

# CHAPTER 11

# BIG NUMBER 65

OFFENSIVE LINEMEN DON'T MAKE the Sports Center highlight reels. They tend not to attract the attention of TV cameras unless they screw up. Like if they let some defender sack their quarterback, or drop a running back for a loss, or if they get flagged for holding or grabbing a face mask, which racks up penalty yards and maybe causes a big play to be called back. But while teams have won Super Bowls without having the best quarterback in the league or the number one running back, top receiver, or pass rusher, there's simply no such thing as a championship team without a stellar offensive line.

They are the five guys mobilized right in front of the quarterback. Their job is to become like a fortress, preventing charging defensive linemen and blitzing linebackers from getting to him on pass plays or to form a human bulldozer to plow down defenders on run plays. They, and their counterparts on the defensive line, are the infantry of a football team – first in on every single play. These are the offensive linemen: The center, who hikes the ball through his legs to the quarterback; the guards, next to the center on his left and his right; and the tackles, just to the outside of each of the guards. Five massive men almost never less than 6-foot-3 and 300 pounds.

They start every offensive play crouched in a three-point stance with one fist planted on the ground and their other forearm resting on a bent knee, still as statues. With the sudden snap of the ball, they explode upward like enraged grizzly bears, growling their way through marauding lineman. Ankles, knees, and quad muscles blast their hulking bodies out of scrunched positions; backs and shoulders thrust forward against opposing forces that can outnumber them or can get a running start at them depending on the play; arms used as battering rams knock enemies out of the way. Helmets crash. It is a titanic clash every time.

There were as many reasons the Panthers were off to a 5-0 start as there were guys on the field and coaches on the sidelines, plus two. Truth was, though, a quarterback who'd only started two games in the NFL had stepped in and led Carolina to a dazzling come-from-behind win over Jacksonville, an overtime win against the Super Bowl champ Buccaneers, wins over division rivals Atlanta and New Orleans, and a second overtime win against Peyton Manning's undefeated Indianapolis Colts. There's no way Jake Delhomme could have done it without first-class protection from big number 65 and the rest of the O-Line.

They had come to be called the Fat Cats, and they were having one heck of a season. You knew they were having a heck of a season by the fact that they'd emerged from the typical under-the-radar path of an offensive line squad to earn that cocky nickname. Their faces would end up fronting cool black T-shirts surrounding a menacing panther with FAT CATS in team blue across the top and CAROLINA'S SPECIAL BREED as the caption. It wasn't just because they were among the most supersized of the Panthers that they'd been dubbed Fat Cats; it was because they'd been playing equally large. With an attitude, swagger, and style usually reserved for celebrity quarterbacks or flashy receivers, the Fat Cats were stars in their own right.

The center, snapping the ball to Jake Delhomme, 6-foot-4-inch, 300-pound Jeff Mitchell. His seventh year in the league. Knew how to get it done and how to win. Starting center for the Super Bowl winning Baltimore Ravens two seasons earlier. Serious practical joker. To Mitchell's left at guard, Jeno James, 6-foot-3, 310 pounds. His fourth season. Big and intense, but the quietest of the Fat Cats with waters running deep. Kept a journal. Wrote poetry to release his deepest thoughts, yet perhaps, the guy you'd most want to have your back in a dark alley.

Outside James at left tackle, Todd Steussie. Solid as a rock at 6-foot-6, 308 pounds. Nine-year veteran. Missed only one game in those nine seasons. Looney as a cartoon in the locker room. The rookie of the bunch, Jordan Gross. A 6-foot-4, 300-pound right tackle. His first season in the NFL, and the most baby-faced guy on the team, but possessing poise and insight far beyond what his 23 years of age and rookie status would suggest.

Between Jeff Mitchell and Jordan Gross at right guard, Kevin Donnalley.

He was the most senior Fat Cat. Twelve years in the NFL. A regional favorite, having played for Davidson College just outside Charlotte before transferring to Chapel Hill to become a University of North Carolina Tar Heel. He entered the NFL as the third-round draft pick of the Houston Oilers in 1991. Became one of the most durable linemen in the league, playing in 187 regular season and playoff games up to that Sunday the Panthers would host Tennessee. One hundred eighty-seven games, 35 plays a game on average. Some 6,500 hand-to-hand clashes in the National Football League, and that didn't include the months of practice every year, the preseason games, or the intra-team scrimmages. Kevin Donnalley was into his thirteenth season, and he had decided it would be his last.

HE WAS ONLY THREE DEGREES of separation from Hope Stout. Emily Rutherford's aunt, Tamara Holt, knew Donnalley's wife, Erica. They had kids in the same school. When Emily's mom, Danette, told her sister Tamara that Hope and Emily would be going to the game and would be down on the field, Tamara immediately called Erica to ask if Kevin could possibly say a quick hello to Hope. She also called an acquaintance in her own neighborhood, Jon Richardson, son of Panthers' owner Jerry Richardson. Along with his brother Mark, he was co-president of the team. Tamara lobbied Jon to intercede. She later had occasion to talk with Kevin directly and ask him herself.

It wasn't something generally done and definitely something *he* didn't do. Through twelve years of professional football Sundays, and four years of college football Saturdays before that, Donnalley had developed a pre-game routine that was sacrosanct almost to the point of obsession. Yet he didn't need dogged persuasion. He was the father of three. His wife had him at *12-year-old girl with cancer*. So when it was also mentioned in the team meeting the morning of the Tennessee game that a girl with cancer would be on the sidelines and would anyone be willing, Donnalley announced he had it covered.

SUNDAY, OCTOBER 19, 2003, was sunny and 69 degrees. The sky was a dreamy Carolina-blue stretching only a smidge wider than Hope Stout's game-day smile. She was bursting with anticipation. Though she detested having to hobble around on crutches, she was feeling better than she had in months and was thrilled to finally be going to see her Panthers. Emily wasn't quite the football fanatic Hope was, but she was jazzed to be there with her on-the-mend friend. It was Emily's first time going to a game, and she wore the same number 90 Julius Peppers jersey as Hope. Emily's was white, and Hope's was the same Panther blue the home team would wear that day. They each had their poster. Emily's declared "Go Panthers" in team colors of blue and black and silver, and it had a big football sailing through a goalpost. Hope's carried a different message.

"DROP the HAMMER on CANCER!" Hope's poster screamed – with Panther paw prints, footballs, and a hammer drawn on it, along with the numbers 58 and 51. Hope knew all about Mark Fields and Sam Mills. She knew all about the team's "Drop the Hammer" campaign. Like many Panther fans, she wanted to show her support. Unlike most, she knew exactly what Sam and Mark were going through. Their battle was also her battle.

As the girls waited outside the stadium with Stuart and Shelby for an escort to take them down to the field, they saw Mark Richardson being whisked inside by an assistant. As he was hustling past the gate, Richardson caught sight of Hope's poster, flashed her a big smile and a thumbs up, and shouted, "That's what we're going to do! We're going to keep on fighting cancer!"

"Yes, we know!" Shelby shot back. "And so are we!"

Her crisp reply stopped the scurrying executive in his tracks. He took in the bandana and crutches and extended right leg of the lanky girl sitting angled in a folding chair while everyone else was standing. Something clicked. To the innocent irritation of an assistant charged with getting her busy boss back to his office on time, Richardson changed course and walked over to Hope. He knelt down next to the chair and looked right into her eyes.

"What's your name?"

"Hope Stout," she replied to Richardson's up-close questioning, not entirely hiding her grin.

"*Heyyy…*" he said, recognition showing. "*I know who you are.*"

Word of Hope had made its way through the organization. From Mark's brother Jon, through Donnalley and the team meeting earlier that morning, and through a staffer who'd gotten Donnalley a Panthers hat to give Hope that Mark and Jon had signed, along with the Big Cat himself – their father, Jerry.

"Listen, I have to be somewhere right now," Richardson said, vindicating his clock-watching assistant, "but I will see you on the field in a few minutes. I want a picture of you and me with that poster."

"Thanks! It took me a couple of hours to draw it," she said, not at all self-consciously.

THE FIELD BEFORE AN NFL GAME is a whirl of activity. Dozens of players are warming up, working out, and running drills; coaches and assistants flow freely between field and sidelines with clip boards, play books, water bottles, and towels and tape. They're talking with players, taking quick meetings, and huddling with each other. Aides set up their team's encampment with headsets, sports-drink stations, medical supplies, exercise bikes, big electric fans, and backup equipment of all kinds.

Just outside the team bench zone is a whole other churning mass of humanity. Staffers from public relations, community relations, marketing, and sales, walk clients, sponsors, and patrons through check presentations, photo ops, and hellos. Blurring the line between the team zone and this *everybody-else* zone lurk former players and celebrities, and TV and radio types who are testing cameras and microphones and trolling for tidbits and stories to drop in during broadcasts.

Hope and Emily were taking all this in with bug-eyes and bright smiles. Two goofy, curious young girls scampering along the sideline – as much as a girl on crutches only two weeks removed from her fifth round of chemotherapy can scamper. She and Emily were digging being down on the field as fans filed in and pre-game tunes pounded out of massive stadium speakers while videos rolled on the Jumbotron and public address announcements echoed. They were pretending they were big shots and imagined people in the stands wondering, *Who are those two very important girls down there?* especially when team president, Mark Richardson, reappeared as promised. He crouched down like a baseball catcher next to Hope, whose pain-racked right leg had by then forced her to give up the scampering and surrender to a chair brought to the sidelines. He draped his arm around her shoulder as their picture was taken.

Inside the stadium, Kevin Donnalley's day had included that morning's team meeting, a meeting of the whole offense, and a meeting of the offensive line. The meetings were separated by time-killing, tension-breaking distractions like bin ball, where basketball-sized wads of tape were tossed into distant laundry bins for sport and dumb frat-boy bets. The Fat Cats goofed around and trash-talked at their lockers. But as the day rolled along, players gradually began to focus and intensify, and Donnalley commenced his pre-game routine.

He stretched, limbered, and stretched some more. He rubbed a personally contrived, disgustingly odorous deep muscle concoction into the knees that carried his 310 pounds through those previous 187 NFL Sundays and into the shoulders that hinged bulging arms for those 6,500 clashes with defenders. He pulled on knee wraps and game pants with thigh pads and layers of socks; then cleats, elbow pads, arm bands, and shoulder pads. Just before the shoulder pads, that T-shirt. Finally, he pulled on his big number 65 jersey. Double XL – and players' sizes run large. Donnalley then set about turning his massive hands into those enormous mitten-clubs.

First, several twists of a blue pre-wrap were followed by white cloth athletic tape wound over the wrists to brace them. Thick leather gloves with wide Velcro wrist bands were pulled on and strapped tight. Blue pre-wrap was wound around just the thumbs. A brace laid on the back of each thumb to keep it from being snapped off by defenders was gripped with more pre-wrap. The entire thumb, palm, and wrist were then twisted up in the blue before being mummified in layers of elastic tape. Then the whole wrist, hand, and braced thumb were encased by rounds and rounds of the white cloth stuff. Ten tedious minutes of taping – when you're a rookie. Donnalley had it down to less than two and a half minutes per hand. Pre-game culminated in the veteran lineman sitting silently for several minutes in front of his own locker, in full gear and uniform, taped up and gloved up, hands holding helmet, forearms resting on wrapped knees, eyes closed and head bowed in prayer, meditation, and graphic visualization of the battle at hand.

This was the Kevin Donnalley who thundered out of the locker room, through the tunnel, and onto the gleaming green grass of Panther Stadium on Sunday, October 19, 2003, as tens of thousands of fans were streaming into the stands. Game face was on. He did calisthenics with the team and drills with the O-Line. A beast came alive inside him. Alive, though restrained. He was ready. Then he broke away when grabbed on the arm by a staffer who led him to the quickie little meet-and-greet, photo-op favor for a friend.

Several minutes later, he would have to be grabbed by the arm again and dragged back to the team.

THE FIRST THING HE NOTICED was the red hair, and the first thought it made him think was of his own red-headed daughter, Kayla, though Hope's hair was a redder red than hers. Hope had fretted over how the wig looked that day. It drove her crazy not being "normal." It was bad enough needing the crutches; she desperately wanted her hair to look real. It did. She was instantly captivating there on the sidelines in her bright-blue Panther jersey, colors matching his, that black bandana, and a white scarf looped casually perfect around her neck. She was tall and thin, smiling and laughing with Emily. Hope, veteran Panther fan that she was, was trying to be cool. First-timer Emily, was amazed by it all. Especially Donnalley. As he approached, her eyes widened.

*He's huge!* she thought.

Donnalley's eyes took a snapshot of the scene and of Hope. He knew, of course, he'd never met her, but the heart pounding inside big number 65 knew a truth greater than the mere facts, and *father's daughter* was the feeling that pulsed through him with each step.

*Cancer*

*Kayla*

*Cancer*

*What if?*

He had squared off eyeball to eyeball with 300-pound pro football linemen set on ripping through him, but this was far more intimidating.

*What do I say?*

The thought didn't linger long, as with his next stride, Donnalley stepped over the white sideline stripe. Before he could figure out what to say, he was saying, "Hi Hope, I'm Kevin Donnalley."

In a moment that was so rare Shelby and Stuart, and maybe even Emily, couldn't believe what they were seeing, Hope was speechless. It had taken a 6-foot-5-plus (in cleats), 310-pound mountain of a man in full football armor walking off the field and *rightuptoher* to catch Hope Stout a little off guard.

"Uh…"

Nervous girly giggles from Hope and Emily. Donnalley was now fine.

"Hi!" Hope finally blurted. "How are you doing?"

"I'm fine. Getting ready for the game. Are you having a good time? I like your sign!"

"Thanks! I worked on it a couple hours. We want to get on TV!"

Hope introduced Emily to Kevin. "Hey, I know your aunt!" Emily was dazed by how nice the gigantic star was.

After those few unusual seconds of being the one lost for words, 12-year-old *SpongeBob SquarePants*-watching Hope Stout, and 35-year-old veteran NFL offensive lineman Kevin Donnalley, began to talk effortlessly about wanting to be on television (she did, he didn't), about football and the Panthers, and about how she was doing. Before anyone realized it, the quickie little meet-and-greet, photo-op favor for a friend had turned into a several minute conversation. Donnalley had lost track of time, but the staffer hadn't and reappeared to grab him. There did happen to be a game about to start. Along with the staffer arrived the team's photographer and Sir Purr, the furry costumed Panther mascot. Pictures were quickly snapped. Donnalley gave Hope a souvenir: the gloves he had worn the game before.

"They're kinda stinky and sweaty, but I signed them for you."

"Cool! Thanks!"

Donnalley had met plenty of fans, even plenty of kids, in twelve years as an NFL star, but those meetings didn't end like this. The giant lineman bent down to give the little girl a gigantic, gentle hug.

"Hope, I love your poster, and that's what I want you to do. Just keep on fighting and getting better. I will be praying for you."

"Thank you."

He rose up from his crouching hug slowly and deliberately. Nothing like the way he'd be rising up from his crouching stance across from some snarling defensive lineman in just a few minutes. With a permission-seeking glance to Stuart, he asked a question he'd never asked before at the close of a meet-and-greet.

"Hope, if it's okay, I'll call you next week to see how you're doing?"

Holding back his pride, his happiness, and his tears – or at least his happiness and pride – Stuart returned a permission-granting nod, which was good, since Hope was already saying, "Sure!" Donnalley turned and trotted back to the team. Stuart and Shelby, a still-astonished Emily, and a beaming Hope were taken to their fabulous seats.

With 69,410 other frenzied fans on that magnificent, magical Sunday in Charlotte, they watched Hope's new best friend and his 5-0 Carolina Panthers get trounced by the Tennessee Titans.

# THAT SEASON OF HOPE

# PART II

## CHAPTER 12

# THE RADIO GUY

I NEVER MAIL IT IN. The radio show. Hate that phrase and hate the very idea, but come on. It was Friday, December 19, 2003, and only three shows stood between me and a thirteen-day Christmas vacation. The world, news, politics, and just plain life my show is made of were all settling in for a long winter's nap. Barring catastrophe, I knew quite well where the year's last nine hours of radio were headed, starting with that day's three.

John Whitehead would be on. Not a household name, but should be. He's one of America's most relentless fighters for our First Amendment freedoms. John is a constitutional lawyer who founded the Rutherford Institute, and I love talking with him because he gets under everybody's skin. By fighting right down the line for the First Amendment, he sounds too conservative for the liberals, too liberal for the conservatives, and ticks off partisans sporting Republican *and* Democratic jerseys. My kind of guy.

There would be the annual chat with Doc Elmo. With his wife, Patsy, Elmo rocked the Christmas world in 1979 with the tune everyone either loves or hates, "Grandma Got Run Over by a Reindeer." Elmo Shropshire, 67 years old and a sweetheart of a guy. Doc's a complete hoot, every year telling in his unmistakable squeaky, smiling voice how as a practicing veterinarian he came to record "Grandma."

And some notes were made for a Friday wrap-up of the biggest story of the week in the Carolinas. The long-whispered rumor was confirmed. When he was young, the late Strom Thurmond had fathered a child by a black teenaged housekeeper who worked in his parents' home. He had kept the tryst and the biracial love child it birthed secret during his 47 years as U.S. Senator from South Carolina, and his 1948 run for president as the candidate of the segregationist Dixiecrat Party. Nothing's more fun than the chance to rile up a small but strident slice of the audience. A good thwacking of the now undeniable hypocrisy of the beloved J. Strom Thurmond, and the phone calls afterward, would be priceless.

I never mail it in, but maybe I did have an envelope addressed as I climbed into the car. Pulling out of the garage into the cool darkness of 5:29 in the morning, I was off on my highly-refined, smooth-as-silk, never-miss-a-mark, fully-autopilot drive to work and show-prep routine.

At the end of the driveway I stopped for my *Charlotte Observer*. The radio was clicked on to 50,000-watt WBT AM/FM. It's the third-oldest station in the country, the "Great Colossus of the South," as it was known back when people used words like colossus. The station is clearly as wise as it is legendary: it employs *me* after all. The first sip of coffee was taken while heading out of the cul-de-sac to start the precisely thirty-minute drive as John Stokes, our iconic veteran news anchor with the conversational baritone, ran down the headlines.

"...It's 5:30 on December 19th and North Carolina health officials say the flu is three times more widespread now than during its usual peak in February...

"...U.S. Administrator in Iraq, Paul Bremer, escapes a close call when his convoy comes under attack...

"...And snow is piling up in the North Carolina mountains where a winter storm warning remains in effect. Partly cloudy and 46 today...."

Nothing in John's update that morning changed the sketch of the program running through my mind, so I licked the stamp and slapped it on the already-addressed envelope of the radio show I was not mailing in. I arrived at the rambling, loveable old studios of WBT and television station WBTV at 6:02. Thirty-*three* minutes. Hit a couple lights.

At the main employee parking lot, I waved the magnetic ID in my wallet over the mysterious little black pad triggering the gate to open. While waiting, I tossed my cell phone into my beat-to-hell, 12-year-old, olive-drab, canvas Land's End briefcase; grabbed the newspaper and... Newspaper hadn't been opened for the normal quick check in the cul-de-sac. I started to flip it open, but the gate began beeping it was clear, and car lights were hitting my rearview mirror. Max, a producer for our sister station, WLNK-FM, was INCH-ING-UP right behind me. He had to be in his studio two minutes ago. I jammed the paper in the briefcase and blasted through.

I grabbed the briefcase and coffee, jumped out of the car, walked under the glow of the flashing red lights of the WBT relay tower, past the fenced-off helipad where the TV news chopper sleeps, and up the ramp of the loading dock. Entering through the door behind the main TV news studio, I walked down the hall to the radio wing past the big picture window of the main WBT studio where the morning news crew was into their second hour and then past the WLNK-FM studio.

Max was already at the controls. He got in ahead of me because he used the corporate-type employee entrance. It's a closer park and shorter walk to the radio wing, but it doesn't have the charm of the stroll beneath the transmitter tower, through the dock, and past all the big old TV and radio studios. I deliberately choose that path every morning even though it takes a little longer. I love what I do and where I work, and this way in warms me with history and heritage even on the coldest, darkest mornings.

I got a second cup of coffee and headed to my home downstairs in the suite of luxury offices of the WBT air personalities. Think bullpen of metal cubicles. Flopping the briefcase on the table behind my desk, I fired up the computer, checked my email, and scanned a dozen websites including the *Washington Post, Washington Times, USA Today, Chicago Tribune, Google News* and some wacky special interest sites. I started to bang out the twisted take on the news that kicks things off every day, "My News and You are Welcome to It," while still looking for anything that might trip my trigger enough to change the shape of the show. Nothing did. Friday, December 19, 2003, was set.

The show that's never mailed in was now in the hands of the postal service as I reached for a third cup of coffee, swiveled back toward the table where the briefcase and newspaper lay and – damn. Never did check the paper. That just doesn't happen. Almost two hours later than usual, and with the show set in my mind, I finally flipped it open.

Off the front page leapt a large photo of a little girl with bright-red hair covered by a jade-green bandana, gazing down into the eyes of a tiny gray kitten she was pulling up close to her face. She was smiling but in a pondering, pensive way. Mesmerizing. Finally glancing below the photo, I caught the headline:

# GRANTING HOPE'S WISH — OFFERED ANYTHING, SHE ASKS TO HELP OTHER SICK CHILDREN

I started to read the story by Elizabeth Leland:

When Make-A-Wish Foundation asked 12-year-old Hope Stout what she wanted, instead of answering, Hope asked a question:

"How many children are waiting on wishes?"

"Another 155," they told her.

"My wish," Hope said, "is to help raise money to grant all their wishes."

Stop the mail.

⚬⚬⚬

I LEANED BACK, took a long sip, and read on.

...Hope, who has a rare form of bone cancer called osteosarcoma, is in bed recuperating from radiation.

...her wish has set off a fundraising drive unlike any other by Make-A-Wish.

...the money raised... will pay for a pony for a 5-year-old Newton boy with a rare blood disorder, a trip to Walt Disney World for a 7-year-old Gastonia girl with leukemia (she wants to dance with Cinderella), and a cruise to the Bahamas for a 15-year-old Ellerbe girl with the same cancer as Hope.

...Hope said, from her home in Weddington...

Wait. What?

Two million people in the Charlotte area, yet I had heard of the girl in the photo on the front page. I had no recollection at first, but it came back in a rush as I read "home in Weddington."

There had been a story in the paper about Hope Stout several weeks earlier. It wasn't on the front page, though. It was in the little, local "Neighbors" section, and there was nothing about any wish. It was a small story by the community news reporter about a girl who had cancer and how her friends at Weddington Middle School were rallying around her. A couple days after the story ran, I was sitting around after dinner with my wife, Nancy, and daughters, Hallie and Kendall. As typical school-night talk was ping-ponging around, I mentioned the story. We live in the town next to Weddington, and Kendall attended Weddington Middle. It's a big school, and Kendall, being a year older than Hope, didn't know her but did know *of* her. She said the kids were saying Hope might die.

...The cancer spread...

...The Stouts... are praying for a miracle.

Sitting in the solitude of my chilly basement office in a time warp that had broken the tightly scripted sprint that is preparing each day's show, sipping coffee and feeling its warmth (or was it something else?) come over me, I remembered looking at Kendall that night and thinking, *My daughter is talking about this kid who's got cancer. What if my daughter was the kid that every other kid was telling their parents about? And what would it be like to be the kid with cancer everybody else was talking about?*

Another realization yanked me back to the present. Despite the way those thoughts and feelings had struck me that night around the kitchen table, I hadn't thought about Hope Stout since. Until just now.

The highly-refined, smooth-as-silk, never-miss-a-mark autopilot that guides me every morning from home to work, through my entire show-prep routine, right up to the moment in the studio when the microphone is cracked open and the 50,000 watts of WBT become mine for three hours – somehow glitched. Ever so slightly, ever so subtly, glitched. The newspaper was not scanned at its precisely appointed time before pulling away from the house. It was not read at the designated moment at the station when its contents would have been stirred in with everything else already percolating in those early morning hours. I would have had plenty of time to prepare myself and plan the show in just the right way. But no.

Time doesn't actually warp in time-warp moments, so now it was late; almost show time. I showed the story to my producer, Mark Thomas. He doesn't handle changes in the plan much better than I do. He also doesn't hide his emotions very well. When Mark's thinking it, it shows, and it showed on his face in seconds as he started scanning.

...Once the money is raised, and the wishes granted, Hope wants to be well enough to add one more wish to the list. She would like to have a walk-on part on a TV show.

"...That was my original wish," Hope said, "to be famous."

"Do you... want me to try to... get the..."

"No!"

Mark was a little startled. He's a good producer, goes right for the story, but while Hope and her wish were now all I was thinking about, I could not go where he had already gone.

"What do you want me to do then?"

"They quote a guy in there from Make-A-Wish, Chuck... something. See if you can track him down so I can talk with him at some point. Maybe first hour."

I packed up my papers and headphones and folders, grabbed my coffee, and bolted up the stairs to the studio.

THE PRERECORDED DECLARATION from the big-voiced announcer-guy, **"This is the Keith Larson Show,"** and the sage youthfulness of Ferris Bueller, **"Life moves pretty fast. If you don't stop and look around once in awhile, you could miss it,"** opened the show as always, followed instantly by the ripping rock and roll intro of Eric Clapton's "Motherless Children." The inherently wiseass slide guitar sets the tone perfectly for the radio guy it intros. On Fridays, over Clapton, I rip into a little rock and roll of my own drawn from the headlines of the week.

**"Hey there, Keith Larson here, and** *this* **is the Week that Was.**

**"Welcome to Charlotte –** *we love our new trains*!

**"SaddamHusseinispulledfromhishole – anddisappears again.**

**"And Strom Thurmond didn't want 'em in the swimming pools or the churches — but he sure didn't mind having one down behind the barn, did he?"**

Clapton carried on for a few more bars of his opening lick while I took a gulp of coffee and shuffled a few papers before continuing with mine.

**"News-Talk 11-10 and 99.3 FM, WBT. Keith Larson, gratefully plugging away for another 24 hours. Proof, you** *can return* **from the living dead."**

From the living dead of life under the lash of Jack Daniels and his many relatives, I am proof you can return, and also from the living dead of the Land of Corporate Stupid. I had left an eleven-year radio career behind and stumbled a ways up the ladder of a certain American hamburger icon and one of its larger advertising agencies, gone looking not for my heart's desire, but for the paychecks and stock options that bought a 6,000-square-foot house and everything that went with it. I ended up with a fancy title, a corner office in a tall, shiny building outside Atlanta, and a hole in my heart as big as the house. A guy who had never wanted to do anything other than be on the radio, and had done it, was flying around the country arguing with wealthy men in sans-a-belt slacks about whether Big Macs should be sold for 99 cents each – *OR* – *two* for *two bucks*.

It was a twelve-year eternity out of radio. The hole in my heart finally got so big I didn't fear a crash landing. I took the leap back in 2000 after a series of seeming flukes led to an offer to do afternoons in Huntsville, Alabama, for one-seventh the money I'd been making. With Nance and the girls crossing their fingers but fully behind me, I jumped at the chance. We lost money on the stupid house and our savings dwindled, but by the middle of 2002, I had been called to one of the great radio stations in the country, and we were living comfortably but sanely in the horse country of Waxhaw, south of Charlotte. I open the show every morning with that reminder to myself of just how grateful I am to be alive and sober and doing what I get to do – one day at a time.

With an on-air "Good Morning" to Mark and my engineer Bo Thompson, I got on with riffing "My News" over Don Henley's tune "Dirty Laundry." That day included pointed jabs at everything from certain matters Iraq to plans for a new off-leash dog park in Charlotte. "Making a little healthy trouble for the people in charge – whoever's in charge," I like to say about the show; "a poke-in-the-eye wherever it's deserved," which, after My News, brought me to the beloved, late, South Carolina Senator, Strom Thurmond.

"This week, the truth about Strom. You know what this is? It came clear to me last night. This is the story of a girl who loved her father far more than he loved her. Here's this woman who, about the time she became a teenager, learned who her father was. And then, over time, learned *what* her father was. She watched her father run for office as a blatant racist, watched him campaign for separation of the races, filibuster against civil rights legislation, campaign against the repeal of laws in the South that prevented whites and blacks from marrying. All the while, she knows the truth about him. She knows the hypocrisy of him. But, she also knew what was at stake for him, so she never ratted him out.

"She knew the truth about her father, J. Strom Thurmond, and everything he was, but she put him first. He put her second, at best, which is just so twisted. It is the very nature of parenthood to put *child* first. It comes from within you. But the half-black girl had more love in her heart for the self-serving race baiter than he did for her. Daughter had more love for daddy than daddy did for daughter."

Gee, the phones were ringing.

But I was running late for the 9:30 news, after which, this particular morning, there would be no time to marvel at the moral contortions of the few who still justified J. Strom. I had something else to get to.

## CHAPTER 13

# THE WISH

"THE PICTURE ON THE FRONT PAGE of the *Charlotte Observer* today is of a 12-year-old girl going through very aggressive treatments for cancer."

I was holding the front section of the paper, eyes again locked on the photo.

"She's got a bandana on her head. She's holding her pet cat. The story is by Elizabeth Leland.

"'When Make-A-Wish Foundation asked 12-year-old Hope Stout what she wanted, instead of answering, Hope asked a question. 'How many children are waiting on wishes?' Another 155, they told her. 'My wish,' Hope then said, 'is to help raise money to grant all their wishes.'"

"How's that for tossing it right back at you? Hope has a rare form of bone cancer, which I don't even know that I can pronounce. She's been going through radiation. She's in bed recuperating. So at the moment Make-A-Wish reaches out to the 12-year-old with this very severe, rare bone cancer, she says... apparently not knowing, like with a genie in the bottle... you can't ask for more wishes, right? But Hope's not playing by those rules. She says, *My wish is to grant all the other wishes.* They say it'll cost a million bucks.

"They have a quote in here from Hope. 'My mom and I were talking about Make-A-Wish, and she said some people don't have enough to get a simple wish. I just had to do something.'"

A sip of coffee; an extra breath. Moment enough for another flash through the brain of that family dinner.

"I don't know how you look at pictures like this, read a story like this, and not find yourself consumed by your own gratitude. I find myself consumed with my own gratitude for my own healthy kids who happen to be... two of them... girls. One is three years older than Hope Stout, and the other, a year older."

Back to scanning the newspaper story.

"So the Make-A-Wish people say they're gonna do this. They've got some sort of fundraiser planned in January. JANUARY?"

Bo and Mark snapped to attention. In the quiet that came over the studio after I barked "JANUARY," I heard myself rhythmically tapping my pen on the desk. I didn't realize I had been tapping.

"I know it's ludicrous, so I'm not even proposing this, but the thought that went through my mind was, this is a couple of days before Christmas. These wishes have to be resolved *before* Christmas. This money's *got* to be committed before Christmas."

I was off in my mind, thinking out loud. In front of a microphone.

"That's crazy. But don't you wish you could do it? Not actually grant the wishes... I'm sure that takes time... but the money. I mean, think about if 155 kids who are battling life-threatening illnesses... not just sick, but life-threatening... and they're at that point where they're on a

Make-A-Wish list. If every single one of them could be told *gotcha covered* by Christmas Eve or Christmas morning..."

The tapping seemed to fill every silence.

"It could be done. It's insane, but it could be done.

"Now *that* would be a pretty 'world class' thing.

"Charlotte's always trying to be seen as a 'world class' city. Wouldn't that say more about people, more about an area than, *We've got the new train. We've got the new arena?*"

Tapping and drifting. Mark flagged me and pointed toward my call-screening monitor.

"Well, I can't say I'm surprised to see we've got all our lines lit up with people who want to contribute to Make-A-Wish. Hang on for just a second. Mark has gotten Chuck Coira on the phone. He's with Make-A-Wish. He's mentioned in this story about Hope. I guess he's been working with the family.

"Chuck? How ya doing?"

"Keith, I'll tell you, I'm doing great. I was fortunate enough to be there when Hope asked for this wish. I have some information I'd love to pass on about why Hope did this."

"Go ahead."

"Is that okay?"

"Yeah."

"I've been with Make-A-Wish for six years, and when we ask a child for their wish, it's limited only to their imagination. When Hope was asked that question, her answer was beyond *my* imagination. I had the opportunity to tell Hope I was sorry she had to be in this kind of position before she'd be able to reach out and grant all these wishes."

There was something rather, determined, in the way this guy was speaking.

"She told me she believed her cancer was a gift from God."

He was talking like he was on a mission.

"That she, in her life, would never be able to touch so many other people's lives. And that I... should never feel sorry for her. That this is her gift... and she's going... to share it... with other people."

His voice was quivering.

"I didn't know what to say to her. I'm talking to a 12-year-old who is operating on a level that's... I'm 54 and I... didn't understand it."

Not merely quivering. *Cracking.*

I jumped back in. I didn't want him to lose it.

"Chuck, Mark is telling me that next hour, after 10:30, after John Whitehead who's coming up next, we're going to talk with Hope's dad."

"Stuart? He's an amazing man."

ANOTHER DAY, ANOTHER TIME, John Whitehead would have led to some terrific radio as always. We talked about a North Carolina man who wanted to mail some Christian reading materials to his son in Iraq, but the postal service refused. They didn't want to send anything that would offend Muslims. John's foundation was defending the man's First Amendment right to send the books. We also talked about Alabama's notorious Chief Supreme Court Justice, Roy Moore, who commissioned a two-ton monument to the Ten Commandments and had it wheeled, secretly one night, into the rotunda of the Supreme Court building. Wrong, Whitehead said. It was going too far in the direction of government appearing to establish a religion.

I probably should have apologized to John. I was asking all the right questions, but was only going through the motions. My brain was working, but I'm sure John could tell my heart wasn't in it. It was caught up in the sight of Mark and Bo answering the calls that kept lighting up our six phone lines. I could hear them in the background answering questions.

"Yes, you can go to NCWISH.org and make a donation."

"No, ma'am, I can't take your pledge at this number, but if you call…"

My heart wasn't into it with John because it was absorbing the emails popping up in my inbox that I couldn't keep from scanning even while we were talking:

> From: Chip....@
> Sent: Friday, December 19, 2003 9:58 AM
> Subject: Hope
>
> ---
>
> Get me a tissue and put the link to Make-A-Wish on your site so i can send in some $$.

> From: Flint....@
> Sent: Friday, December 19, 2003 10:01 AM
> Subject: Make-A-Wish
>
> ---
>
> Okay Larson, how do we want to do this thing? I'll take one child or I'll kick in $1,000 in my daughter's name. She is well, married and happy. Her wish has come true.

> From: Rexa....@
> Sent: Friday, December 19, 2003 10:25 AM
> Subject: Hope
>
> ---
>
> Keith: I just put $100 in the mail to Make-A-Wish
>
> Rex

After hanging up with John, I would usually get a fresh cup of coffee and settle in for the kind of 360-degree radio fun I live for: wrestling with callers over Judge "Moses" Moore and the politically correct United States Postal Service. I would instead be talking with a father of three, just like me, except my youngest daughter hadn't been stricken with cancer. As I said goodbye to John and went to the news, I was already living in the next half hour.

What do you say to a man whose little girl may be dying?

"10:33 NOW, AND ON THE PHONE is Stuart Stout, whose daughter is 12-year-old Hope Stout, about whom we've been speaking. Stuart, hello; good morning."

"Good morning, Keith. How are you doing?"

"Well, first off, I know everybody will have the best wishes and thoughts and prayers for Hope, Stuart."

"Thank you. I appreciate that. Believe me, that means so much to our family right now."

"I have daughters and a son... but any of us... it makes you feel like you need to drop to your knees and thank God we're not in the spot you and Hope are in. I hope you know what I mean."

"I do. Absolutely."

"So maybe if you're not in the position Stuart and Hope and their family are, well then maybe you can dial up Make-A-Wish. Stuart, where did this thought of Hope's come from?"

"You know, I can't speak for her, but basically Hope has always been this kind of kid. She's always been the first one to think of other people. When the Make-A-Wish people came to our house, they asked her what her wish would be, and she had visions of being on a TV show or doing a modeling shoot. She wants to be famous, which is not unusual if you know Hope."

"Ha!"

"But she said she wanted to do all that when she got better. So they started talking about the Make-A-Wish family and the 155 kids on their list, and she said, 'That's what I want to do. I want those kids to get their wishes.'"

"So you weren't surprised she would come to that kind of thought?"

"Not at all."

"I know you said you don't want to speak for her, but I'm speaking with you, so I guess you have to."

"Hey, listen; I'm sure she'd love to talk with you. In fact, she's probably a little bit upset I'm talking to you. Feel free! She said she'd love to talk to you. Once you get through with me, call her. I'll be glad to give Mark the number and get her on the air."

"Uhh... well then... we should do that."

"Absolutely."

Stuart may have been certain, but I wasn't.

"I mean, if you're actually saying it's okay to do that... I don't know how to handle these kinds of things, so I don't want to be... I mean... if that's okay with you, and that's okay with her, then that's fine; that would be great."

"You have clearance from the commander to do that. She's the one who's running the ship, believe me. She started this, and the ball started rolling, and we can't stop it."

"Stuart, what is the situation with Hope?"

"She has metastatic osteosarcoma, which is bone cancer that has spread. It typically attacks children between the ages of ten and twenty who have experienced a number of growth spurts and things of that nature.

What happened in her case was she just had some knee pain. We monitored the progression of the pain and went from the pediatrician to the orthopedist, and that's when we found out we had a situation with a possible tumor. Unfortunately, it was a very aggressive type of osteosarcoma we had to deal with."

"Stuart, again, if this is... I don't mean to be so basic as to be stupid, but how are you guys plugging along? How do you deal with this?"

"There's only one thing that's kept us going through this, and that is our faith in God. This family's always been a family of deep faith. And our friends have surrounded us in ways... it's incredible how we've been surrounded. The only thing I can tell you is, you just don't know how to get through things like this. There's just one answer, and that's faith in God. My wife and I and the kids, all of us, have had moments where you hit the wall, and all you can do at that point is hit your knees. At that point, you find out who's in control of the whole situation. That's the answer."

"Stuart, I'm going to take a break here, and I don't know if we'll do this in a few minutes or if we'll do it next hour, but once we find out Hope's okay to talk with us..."

"Sure thing."

"Stuart Stout, I know everybody is going to wish the best and pray the best for you and Hope. I appreciate you talking with us."

"Thank you so much, Keith."

As I went into the break and put Stuart on hold, Mark picked up the line, and I could tell he was getting a number. As he hung up he turned to me with a little "I told you so" look on his face but also uncertainty in his eyes.

"So *now* do you want me to try to get the girl?"

He didn't need an answer.

I glanced at more emails popping up and all my phone lines flashing and scanned the computer monitor with the caller list on it with brief notes behind the first names of people wanting to talk.

"Wants to pledge to Make-A-Wish."

"Go ahead and talk with Hope."

"We can do this!"

In a few seconds more, the break was ending, and I heard Mark saying to someone as I pulled my headphones back on, "11:30?" I watched him listen, then nod, and then in the headphones I heard the recording of the big-voiced announcer-guy again declaring, "This is the Keith Larson Show," and it was back to me. My microphone was on, but I sat motionless as Mark threw his arm high into the air with a "thumbs up" to signal next hour I was going to talk with a 12-year-old girl possibly dying of cancer. Never done that before. I realized I was hearing the bump tune play – and play and play and play – and saw Bo frantically waving the *GO!* cue, and I snapped to.

"KLarson at WBT.com."

"Keith, thanks for bringing The Celebration of Hope to my attention. The check's in the mail. I forgive your snarky remarks about Strom Thurmond. Today's compassion is the real you!"

"Well, wait. So are the snarky comments about Strom! This is not either–or. One does not exclude the other. You can be snarky about Strom and also want these wishes granted."

The segment with Stuart had run long, so now I was already hearing the hourly close music coming up underneath me.

"Next hour, Doc Elmo. And yes, we will speak with Hope Stout."

As we went to the news, the phone lines kept ringing, Bo and Mark kept answering, and the emails kept popping:

From: DSSin....@
Sent: Friday, December 19, 2003 10:38 AM
Subject: Make-A-Wish

---

As I listened to you this morning talk about Make-A-Wish I could not help but think that this season is about "miracles." What an amazing little girl – Let's go for it! If everyone gave one dollar to commemorate each "healthy" person in their family... The Panther game on Sunday would be a great collection point if we could get the word out...

From: Chris....@
Sent: Friday, December 19, 2003 11:04 AM
Subject: Hope Stout

---

Hey Keith–I work with Stuart, and Hope is a special little girl as you will find out when you talk to her. But let's get to the money. I want to challenge all insurance agents to a $500 donation. Thanks.

I walked out of the studio. There was no way to not pick up on the buzz in the halls. Something was happening.

On one level I loved it, in the way I love it when anything I do is connecting with listeners and the phone is ringing and the email is hopping. On another level, this was entirely different. It wasn't just some exploding talk topic or some fabulously deft parrying and thrusting with callers in the pure joy of radio fencing. This was something mysterious but real, and I was doing it, but it didn't feel like I was doing it. It felt like it was happening on its own.

Earlier that morning, when I stumbled across the picture of Hope and read the story, I had felt something come over me the way the sun suddenly but softly blankets you when it reappears from behind the clouds on a spring day. *Hey,* I thought, *maybe we can help raise a little money. Maybe we can get this jump-started by Christmas.* But it wasn't as simple as that. Something was happening. In that radio studio. Around Charlotte. In the Carolinas. It had been less than a couple of hours, but I could feel it.

This was a boat starting to move out over the water. Not because we were pushing the throttle on its outboard, but because a warm, gentle breeze had come upon us. We simply put our sails up and caught it. Or maybe the breeze caught *us* and made us put the sails up. I didn't know, but that breeze was starting to blow us out of the protected waters of the harbor and onto a course only it knew. *If* it even knew.

All *I* knew was the usually commanding captain was not in control of the ship.

THE LAP AROUND THE BUILDING and pit stop slipped by too quickly. In a blink I was back in the studio hearing the hourly show open and the big-voiced announcer-guy once again. Then the uniquely familiar notes of "Jingle Bells" that led into the opening chorus, "Grandma Got Run Over by a Reindeer, walking home from our house Christmas Eve..." A smile cracked knowing that a few laughs with Doc Elmo would be just the suspension of reality I needed to keep me from obsessing about the conversation I was going to have after the 11:30 news. Out of the clip of "Grandma" I launched into the cheesy, fun side of the season.

"All right! Time for our Christmas visit with Doc Elmo himself! Elmo, how you doing?"

"Wonderful, Keith! Good morning!"

The sound of Elmo's squeak of a voice made everyone in the studio smile.

"I want to mention one thing, Dr. Elmo. Hang on with me here one second. About 11:35 we're going to talk with Hope Stout. There is a girl here, Doc, who has a very rare and very serious form of bone cancer, and the Make-A-Wish people went to her and said..."

I recapped the story of Hope and what had been going on that day for the late-morning crowd.

"...So we'll talk with her and have more information about how people can help out. "That'll be coming up. But Doc, you have a new CD out?"

"It's called 'Up Your Chimney.'"

The studio cracked up, and we were off for a half-hour of laughs with Doc. The diversion was grand but still no match for the persistently flashing phone lines, endless emails, or people stopping in the studio whispering questions to Mark or mumbling something to Bo.

Before I knew it I was saying, **"Thanks Doc; talk with you next year,"** and we were going into the news.

**"We'll talk to Hope Stout when we come back."**

## CHAPTER 14

# HOPE EXPLAINS IT ALL

IN WHAT SEEMED LIKE SECONDS, the news was ending, and Bo was asking frantically, "What tune do you want me to play here?" and I was saying, "I don't know; you'll make it right." I was sitting with the Elizabeth Leland story I'd been scribbling notes on all morning and a blank legal pad in front of me, eyes closed. I had never talked with a little girl who might be dying of cancer. I had no idea how to do it or what to say. In my mind flashed the words of the Serenity Prayer that opens every AA meeting, "God, Grant me the serenity to accept the things I cannot change…" In the headphones I suddenly heard Bo, at his best, playing a WBT jingle out of the past that sounded just right for the present with singers singing gently, "Mer-ry Christ-mas… Double-YOU-BEE-TEE" and then big brass horns blowing the opening declarations of the carol, "Joy to the World." As the string section joined in, without any idea what I was about to say, I heard myself over the music…

"All right…"

*With the slightest hesitation.*

"Keith Larson here…"

*A touch of tentativeness.*

"...and we have on the phone with us a 12-year-old girl who..."

*Only a toe in the water at first, but I knew I had to just...*

"...had a big idea... as we've been talking about this morning,"

*...jump right in.*

"Hope Stout was given the opportunity to have a wish fulfilled by the Make-A-Wish people. She said, *I want to fulfill the wishes of the other people on your list, the other kids on the list.* An amazing story, and the Make-A-Wish people decided they're going to go ahead and do that. In reading about this, this morning, and actually having been aware to some extent of Hope previously, we said, *Hey, it sure seems like Charlotte oughta be able to come up with this million bucks,* as insane a thought as it is, maybe even by Christmas, so Hope could get her wish as a Christmas present. And as importantly, more importantly, these other kids could get their wishes, or at least know they're going to happen for certain, as a Christmas present.

"So, that's the story. And Hope Stout is on the phone. Hello, Hope."

In the next instant, I heard for the very first time, the bright, optimistic, young voice of Hope Stout.

"Hello! How are you doing?"

"I'm doing... uh... I'm doing fine. Thank you for being with us on WBT today. Your dad, earlier, said it was okay that we talk with you, so I appreciate you talking with us."

"Thank you for having me on."

*She's* thanking *me?*

"Uh... Hope... how... You have... a form of a bone cancer?"

"Yes, sir."

And for a few moments we both shifted into a careful interview mode.

"And you've been dealing with this for five or six months now?"

"Mm hm. Yes."

"And the Make-A-Wish people came and brought the opportunity to you to have a wish fulfilled, and I've relayed what you said to them, but tell me how that happened. Tell me, where did this thought come from?"

"Well, it just came from being in the hospital and getting my treatments, and I saw all these other kids, and they... they were so... they just seemed so happy in there, and they didn't know what was going on. They were just running around with their little IV poles and stuff, and then I found out some of them aren't nearly as lucky as me because I had my parents there by me 24/7, and some of them didn't have their parents there because they lived in another state or something."

In seconds, as her thoughts went back to the hospital and the other kids, Hope gained strength and confidence in her voice. The honesty of her heart was instantly evident. She was leading us through a surreal conversation with a passion and wisdom and insight that couldn't possibly have been coming from a 12-year-old girl.

"And all they're asking is to meet Ronald McDonald or go on a cruise, and it seemed so easy to do... and it broke my heart some kids don't get the chance to do all this great stuff because I have the opportunity to go to, like, Cancun. I just had to do something about that. I couldn't live with myself knowing these little kids are asking for so little and maybe not getting the chance to get it."

"And Hope, some of those wishes from Make-A-Wish, the Ronald McDonald variety, you're right, those aren't even so much about big money, are they? That's just about making some arrangements. Of course, for 155 kids, that will run into some money. The Make-A-Wish people figure that could cost a million bucks. We've heard from a bunch of people here today, Hope, that are blown away by this thought you had, *What I want is for these wishes to happen for these other kids.* I think you've inspired a lot of people around the area today. Are you aware of that?"

"Yes, I am. It's amazing how many people are so inspired by me, but all I'm doing really, is sitting in bed all day watching TV and caring about these other kids. And just to see their smile and to know I made a difference in their lives is an amazing feeling. It's far better than any other wish, like to go to the Bahamas or something or to be famous. It's... That feeling you get to know you made a difference in some kid's life... is just... amazing!"

This was a 12-year-old girl I was talking to.

"And you say you're at home, Hope? When's the last time you were at school?"

"I have not been to school at all this year. I'm doing home school, and I have my teachers come, and they give me the work and stuff. But as of this year, I have not been in the seventh grade."

"And you're going through radiation treatments?"

"Yes, I recently went through those just a few weeks ago. I want to say thank you to all the radiationists down there. They were so nice and so caring and came up every day to see how I was feeling. And the nurses who took time out of their breaks to come and see me and see how I was feeling... They're so sweet, and I want to take this time to say thank you. They've made the stays in the hospital so much more enjoyable."

I could not believe this was a 12-year-old-girl.

"And you're saying you've got your parents and sisters and family around you, and that helped you to have this thought to be thinking of other kids, and you told me about your experience, seeing the other kids, but where did that thought come from do you think?"

"My mom is a caring person, and when she was staying in the hospital, she would go find out about other people who were in there and see what their story was. I heard some of them were alone in the room and didn't have their parents there because their parents had to work to pay off medical supplies. And I honestly cannot see myself fighting this cancer without my parents there 'cause they think they do so little, but they have no idea how much they do. Whether it's handing me the remote, going down to get me a snack... It means so much to me just to have them there, and the thought of some little kid who's younger than me who could be going through something worse, alone, but still having the faith is... amazing. I want to do whatever I can to make their stay as good as it can be.""That's a big part of it, faith, isn't it?"

"Mm Hm. This is all coming from faith in God. None of this, not one part of this, would be happening if we did not have God in our lives. He's just... My relationship with... How I've grown with Him is... It's unexplainable how I can find myself starting up a conversation with God saying, 'Thank you for making this day easy for me, and be with all the other ones in pain who have it so much worse than me and may not live to see next year.' And their big wish is to have a puppy or go to LEGOLAND. I have to make sure these kids get their wishes. It's just... It's *going* to happen. I know with the power of God, and with all these people who are hearing about this, I *know* this can happen; one hundred percent. I know we can do *so* much more, but I have one-hundred-percent faith in God. We're just giving it all to Him, and He's going to take care of it."

"Well, a lot of people are responding to that idea of yours, Hope, to grant your wish, which is to grant the wishes of the 155 other kids. We've been amazed at the response we've heard today talking about this, and then talking with Chuck from Make-A-Wish and your dad last hour, the people calling and telling us, *You know it's crazy, but not only can all these wishes happen and this money be raised, but it's got to be able to happen in a few days so it can be a Christmas gift.* Even if all the actual wishes don't happen, the other kids could know for Christmas these things are gonna happen for them. It's great."

It was great, and she was great, and we were rolling. We'd been talking almost ten minutes, and muscle memory had taken over. Good thing. I was feeling rattled by this little girl who had done nothing but tell her story and reveal her true heart and spirit; the truth in her heart giving so much strength to her voice. Yet as the minutes wore on, a breathiness came along. Barely detectable at first, a deliberate, gasping struggle to inhale contrasted with the effortless way she opened herself up.

And did she hear herself? Did she hear when I asked about her treatments? I could only imagine how brutal they must be for anyone, let alone a little girl, and the first thing she said about them was, "Thank you to all the radiationists down there who were so nice and so caring." Did she realize how instinctively she put others first? Did she hear the gratitude in her voice when she talked of thanking God for making the day easy for her? Did she realize the very first moment the increasing labor of working for a breath became evident was when she was talking about how easy her own ordeal was? Did she hear the concern when she spoke of all the other children who may not live to see next year? Did she comprehend the irony?

I was a guy who'd spent the last ten minutes of his 45-year-old life in a conversation with a 12-year-old girl who may have been losing hers, and she had reached right through the headphones, straight to my heart, and grabbed me. I was at the edge. Thank God that while Hope had grabbed my heart, it was my head and reflexes managing the conversation, or I might have lost it.

It was a couple of minutes past the time I was supposed to break. Out of the corner of my eye, I saw CHUCK COIRA on the call screen. I knew I needed to get to the commercials if I was going to get back to him for an update and complete the circle of this show, so I shifted into wrap-up mode with Hope, breathing a huge sigh of relief knowing I'd made it.

"You're an amazing person. You've inspired a lot of people today, and prior to today... but I know today you have... and I really appreciate your time and telling your story. I'm sure you're going to get a lot of response to the Make-A-Wish office with a lot of pledges and a lot of money to make this happen over the next few days."

"Yes. I'm telling everybody trust in God and believe in yourself and anything is possible. I have one-hundred-percent faith we can make these kids' wishes come true, and then my wish can come true. I mean, my first wish was to be famous and have a walk-on role on a TV show, but that's already happening. I mean from you calling me and wanting to talk... This is all I need right now, and then to have these kids' wishes come true. I know we can do it. Just have one-hundred-percent faith in God, and anything can happen."

What? She off-hands her first wish was to be famous, "but that's already happening" from me calling her and wanting to talk? *This* is all she needs right now? Ahh Shit. Shit.

"The... uh... Make-A-Wish phone number is 704-339-0334. The website... NC.wish.org. We have both of those linked up to the Larson page at WBT.com. Hope Stout, thanks again. You're amazing. I know a lot of people, all of us here, but a lot of people are grateful for what you're doing and are praying for these other kids and, especially, praying for you today as well. I really appreciate talking with you."

Phew. Done.

"Thank you for having me on the show. It's a big honor!"

BAM.

"Uhh..."

Sacked. Stomped on the chest, clutched at the throat, and broken wide open by a little girl lying in bed grabbing grown men by the hearts (I would hear from many), as without a thought of the metaphor, she was giving what may be left of her life to others.

"Well..." Desperate exhale.

Inhale.

Clearing throat.

"I..."

Swallowing.

"I don't know about that, but hopefully we raise the money... uh... Hope."

Hanging on. Barely.

"And thanks for talking with us."

"Okay! Thank you for having me."

"Okay."

Voice cracking entirely, losing it hopelessly, I rushed to the break.

"We'll be back."

Hope Stout. "Mesmerizing." Page 100
Charlotte Observer Photo

Jake Delhomme. "Boyishly Boundless." Page 19
Charlotte Observer Photo

Hope's Calendar. October 17-19, 2003.
"Weekend of a Lifetime." Page 80

Hope "Knew exactly what Sam and Mark were going
through." With Emily Rutherford. Page 87

Hope meets Kevin Donnalley. With Stuart Stout.
"He's Huge!" Page 91. Charlotte Observer Photo

Hope at home, with Shelby and Stuart Stout;
and Kevin Donnalley. "The Halloween visit in
particular perked Hope up." Page 158

Steve Smith. "Elation!" Page 213. Charlotte Observer Photo

Stuart, Holly, Shelby Stout; Kevin Donnalley. Rally
before NFC championship. "There was no clear line
between the Carolina Panthers and Hope Stout's
wish." Page 220. Charlotte Observer Photo

Kevin Donnalley, 65, Jake Delhomme, 17, and the Carolina Panthers take the field at Houston's Reliant Stadium. "It was one of the great Super Bowl games of all time. But no one much remembers." Page 247 Charlotte Observer Photo

Hope Stout. Sixth grade picture. "5-B." Page 189

# CHAPTER 15

# BRUSH FIRE

"KLARSON AT WBT.COM"

Back on the air Monday morning, December 22.

"I got this email about the middle of the afternoon Friday. 'She got to you, didn't she? She's only been doing that to me for about twelve years or so.'

"This is from Hope Stout's dad, who was thanking us – ha! thanking *us* – for the opportunity to be on the show. He says, 'You have no idea what an impact the show's had, having Hope on and telling people to get involved in her wish.'"

Actually, I did have some idea.

When the show ended shortly after talking with Hope, minutes after I'd been broken by a girl who wasn't trying to break anyone, people in the building didn't know how to react. Several had gathered near the big viewing window into the studio as I talked with her and listened on the speakers in the hall. They didn't stand right up to the glass like the tour groups do, making me feel the way a chimp in the monkey house must feel. They stood back and were careful not to stare, not to make eye contact or distract me; but I could sense them hovering. The way the conversation ended, I could feel the jolt that hit them. They couldn't believe what they had heard. There was no *crying* on *my* show. There was no *losing* it to a little girl. People smiled or gave me a look, but didn't say anything. Which was good. Them not saying anything meant that I didn't have to try to say anything back. Yet even in their silence, I heard them loud and clear. I heard all weekend from people who had heard Hope.

> From: Dunn....@
> Sent: Friday, December 19, 2003 2:16 PM
> Subject: HOPE!
>
> _____
>
> Doesn't this kid Hope know you shouldn't make grown men cry?

> From: Will....@
> Sent: Friday, December 19, 2003 3:17 PM
> Subject: Friday's show
>
> _____
>
> A check will be in the mail. How does a family raise a 12-year-old of that caliber? I was raised by fine parents but at 12, was a nitwit. Guess I just never had to bear that kind of burden.

> From: jbea....@
> Sent: Friday, December 19, 2003 9:51 PM
>
> _____
>
> dear keith, i would just like to yell at you!!! i am listening to John Hancock, and he just replayed your interview with hope stout. i was having the best pity party i have had in a long time. believe it or not i just told my daughter that this was the worst day i have ever had. and then i hear Hope, literally!!! it is amazing how we sit in our own little worlds even at a time of the year like this. i am so ashamed of myself. at this time i cannot give money, but i will be asking for donations from my church. i get paid

quarterly and i will be donating as soon as i can. i am only
sorry i cannot do more!! thank you so very much for this.

Our afternoon drive guys had talked about my conversation with Hope and her wish, and they kept pumping the Make-A-Wish info. Hancock did more than talk. John is our evening guy and had heard Hope on Friday morning. She had roped his heart just as she had mine and so many others. He'd been getting calls and emails about her from listeners and decided to play the whole conversation back. Twice. In his first hour – which on top of being part of a typically busy Friday drive home, was also part of the last-Friday-before-Christmas shopping rush – and again late in his show, when the sun is down and the moon is up and the 50,000 watts of WBT are booming from Canada to Cuba.

Saturday morning in the *Charlotte Observer*, Elizabeth Leland had an update:

## HOPE FUNDRAISER FOR WISHES
## OFF TO FAST START
## 12-year-old: I HAVE 100% FAITH

People in the Carolinas are helping
  make Hope's wish come true.


…Phone calls flooded Make-A-Wish Foundation.

…"It's amazing," said Bruce Lawrence, regional director of Make-A-Wish.

…"I'm just telling everybody if you trust in God and believe in yourself, anything is possible," Hope told Keith Larson on WBT 1110 AM. "I have 100% faith we can make these kids' wishes come true."

The Carolinas had started getting wrapped up in Hope. The *something* I thought I could feel happening as Friday's show unfolded, absolutely was. Monday and Tuesday, those last two days and last two shows before Christmas vacation, sort of rolled into one.

"I was thinking, coming in today, *Okay, let's see... the swirl over Charlotte's new train? Some other nonsense going on somewhere?* We're here these last two days before the holidays, and we'll do some normal things, but there's nothing I'm interested in as much as seeing if there aren't ways to keep elevating this and raise more money for the purpose of granting Hope Stout's wish. There's just not much else that feels important these last two days I'm here before Christmas vacation, so that's what we'll do."

And that's just what we did.

I had a year-end talk with a regular on the show, William Kristol, founder of *The Weekly Standard* magazine and Fox News Channel contributor. The past year or so, we had done some serious fencing over the matter of Iraq, Kristol and me. He was all for going in; me, not so much. Bill Kristol is one of the most objective and cordial fencers I've come across, and though he was a big supporter of the invasion, he was not shy about saying where he thought President George W. Bush had made mistakes. Iraq was the story of the year, and I appreciated having him on again.

We had our annual Jimmy Buffet Christmas CD day, when we play Buffet's tropics-infused holiday tunes like "Ho Ho Ho and a Bottle of Rum" and "Christmas Island." I took a call from iconic professional wrestler Ric "Nature Boy" Flair, who lives in Charlotte, and who was involved with the upcoming college football bowl game at Panther Stadium. And I served up "My News and You are Welcome to It" to start each show as always. Mostly though, we talked about Hope – after I played back the conversation with her again myself.

"We've gotten a BUNCH of emails from you guys... people who've donated, people challenging other people to donate. A lot of people writing and talking about Hope after hearing her. Most of those emails, I probably won't be reading. They're nice, touching emails, but there's no way for me to make it through them.

"As we started Friday, I had no idea how to raise a million bucks in a few, or even several, days. There's no traditional math that does it. It can't happen by any conventional means. It has to become exponential somehow. Like in your church on Christmas Eve, the way you light all the candles off of one. So we need some exponential stuff happening. We need some TV news stories. I happen to know the stations are having their story meetings – the, *Hey, what are we going to cover today?* meetings – right now. It would be good if they would go do some follow-up story about Hope. It doesn't have to involve any of this conversation. Just go do your own thing. Make it your own, because that'll touch a bunch of people. I mean, we talk to a lot of people here, thousands in the Carolinas, but this is just one radio station. This is traditional mathematics. We need exponential. So it would be great if all the TV stations would pick up on this. And the other newspapers. And the other radio stations.

"We also need to bag a few elephants. I don't know how we do that. I'm open to any thoughts on how we do that, but we need to bag a few elephants too. We need somebody from NASCAR, or we need one of the big bankers in town or somebody to stand up and say: *Here's twenty-five Gs. Here's fifty.* Really large! We've got to bag a few elephants."

Mark had gotten Chuck Coira from Make-A-Wish on the phone for an update.

"Chuck, how are things going?"

"Keith, we have granted seventeen wishes since you began this Friday. It normally takes a month and a half to do something like that. It has overwhelmed us."

"That would be considered a good response?"

"It would be considered absurd."

"Well I'm looking for even more absurd than that."

"You and me both."

"What does that mean in terms of money?"

"In terms of contributions, it's nearly $100,000. Saturday we came into our office and we had 238 envelopes, all with contributions in them. We had a fella call in who heard you and Hope and sent us a check for $1,110." (WBT's dial position)

"Jeez."

"We had a family come in here Saturday. They had a trip to go to Disney. They heard Hope on Friday, and they have cancelled their trip to Disney World. It was a family decision, and they have donated $5,000 to grant Hope's wish."

"Are you serious?"

"Yeah."

"So 155 minus 17..."

"It's 138 wishes."

Seventeen wishes granted since Friday. What did that mean?

Make-A-Wish doesn't "grant" a wish until the money for it is committed, either by family and friends, or until general fundraising efforts bring in enough to cover it. The wish director is constantly balancing the length of time a wish has been on the list, with the medical conditions of the kids, in deciding which will be granted next. Then there are wishes that must be acted on urgently based on a doctor's assessment. They are called "rush wishes." With money from Hope's wish starting to roll in, they were already starting to give kids who'd been on the list awhile the good news and also scramble to grant some rush wishes.

Granting 155 wishes represented almost a year and a half of raising money and granting wishes for the Charlotte chapter. Hope had made a wish that was going to require a year and a half's worth of fundraising to happen in just a few days; at most, a few weeks. It was probably Providence that I didn't comprehend the size of the mountain until we were already climbing it.

"There's just not much in the heart today, mine and most of yours, I know, other than Hope and her wish... a 12-year-old girl who's got a really serious form of bone cancer, and her wish is to grant all the other kids' wishes.

"That's the power behind this whole thing. This isn't some, *Hey get on the phones,* radio thing. This unfolded itself. That's what's powerful about it. It's this very different, very honest true story, and we find out about it during the Christmas season. It's this girl giving of herself, selflessly, to others. Her thought, at the most challenging time any human being could imagine, let alone a 12-year-old, is of others.

"And this isn't a story in some Christmastime book or movie or something. This is real life; actual real life, right from the mind and heart of this little girl. Although she'll tell you, as she told us Friday, this isn't a thought of her own. This thought has been placed into her from outside of her. This is a thought from God, as she describes it. She's just being a channel and carrying this message.

Her reaction to it all, to her place in it, is not just very, but abnormally humble and understated. So you come across this story and this girl, and how can you help but be affected by it? And infected by it, and respond to it in some way?"

IN SOME WAY? In wondrous ways. People were being affected by Hope and responding. With money, of course. Yet what was going on, what this fabulous infection of Hope was doing in people, went beyond money.

> From: kcyo....@
> Sent: Tuesday, December 23, 2003 11:59 AM
> Subject: Merry Christmas
>
> ---
>
> Hi Keith. Just wanted to take the time to wish you and yours a very Merry Christmas. The past few days have touched me seeing all the response to Hope's wish. I have seen the true meaning of Santa Claus!
>
> From: bbus....@
> Sent: Tuesday, December 23, 2003 1:23 PM
> Subject: For Hope
>
> ---
>
> I saw a shooting star last night, it reminded me of you.
> It was so beautiful and bright, almost too good to be true.
> I closed my eyes and made a wish, that your wish would come true

One does not tire of reading beautiful email after beautiful email from people anxious to confirm to themselves, by reaching out and telling you, how they'd been touched by Hope. Still, there was the reality of needing to raise a million dollars as fast as possible, so the ones that mentioned money were also welcome.

> From: MedD....@
> Sent: Monday, December 22, 2003 7:18 PM
> Subject: Hope
>
> ---
>
> Keith, I wanted you to know that my family and I have just sent in a donation for $1000, to help toward the goal. I was touched – as a listener, a Christian, a cancer survivor and a dad with a 12-year-old girl – by Hope and her unselfishness and her courage.
> Merry Christmas.

Yet even among the contribution emails, the richest were not necessarily those pledging the most money.

> From: Sher....@
> Sent: Tuesday, December 23, 2003 3:26 PM
> Subject: Hope
>
> ---
>
> Keith, My 8- and 6-year-olds were taken by Hope's story and have made their $8.50 and $1 pledge, respectively, which probably represents 20% of the money they get during the year.
>
> Sheri

And just like in church on Christmas, candles being lit by Hope were lighting other candles.

A guy emailed saying he'd heard me talk about needing to spread the story of Hope's wish exponentially, so he had written about it on a blog he runs and posted links to the Make-A-Wish and Celebration of Hope websites. He said he didn't know how much difference it would make, but he figured it couldn't hurt.

A freelance writer who had once interviewed me emailed that she'd heard Hope and was moved to tell others any way she could. She had called New Life 91.9 radio and told them Hope's story. That station's morning guy, Gary Morland, would be interviewing Stuart Stout to get the word out. Down the hall in our own building, at CBS affiliate WBTV, Molly Grantham's candle had been lit, and she was ready to light many others. Her story was the lead on Monday's five and eleven o'clock news:

**"Hope Stout is quickly becoming an inspiration to thousands of people. She was an outgoing, spirited, healthy teenager until June when she was diagnosed with a rare form of bone cancer. Make-A-Wish called asking what she wanted. Hope's wish: to grant the wishes of the other 155 kids on their list."**

Molly had hustled to the Stout home and interviewed Stuart. He smiled as he described his basketball-playing, cheer-leading, do-just-about-anything-she-wanted-to-do daughter, and beamed a bit self-consciously when he told Molly his reaction when Hope made her wish.

**"You know when she said what she said... uhhh... I just thought, well, that's par for the course."**

But Stuart's joy couldn't hide his fear as he allowed that Hope, just then, was having a little difficulty. Molly was unable to talk with Hope herself, so she used clips from Hope's conversation on the radio.

**"...Caring about these other kids, and just to see their smile and to know I made a difference in their lives is an amazing feeling. It's far better than any other wish...**

**"...I know we can do it. Just have one-hundred-percent faith in God and anything can happen..."**

And she interviewed me.

"Talking to Hope on the air, the thing that strikes you is she is so clear in the goal and mission that she wants to grant these wishes for these other kids."

Stuart had given Molly several pictures. There was Hope playing with a big dog, and Hope sandwiched between two redheaded cousins. There was Hope posing with Stuart and her uncle that fabulous week at the beach after her diagnosis but before her chemo began – the blazing red hair still her own – looking strong, as though she hadn't a care in the world. But for the crutches she leaned on to keep the weight off her knee, the picture offered no hint of the attack cancer had launched inside her, or the battle that would soon come. And there was Hope, in her Panther jersey and white scarf, with her dad and the team's fuzzy mascot, Sir Purr, on the field before the Tennessee game, her hair now the red wig under the ever-present bandana, her face thinner. The pictures from the beach and the Panther game perfectly framed Hope's eighty-day pounding from cancer and chemo. In both she smiled widely.

Molly's TV story gave glimpses of Hope differently than a newspaper piece could or than I could. It pulled her face and voice and plight, and her family and faith and wish, and the radio guy and the Fat Cat and the Panthers, all together. It was the first of many stories about Hope that would come from Molly Grantham. Candles lighting other candles had started a brush fire in the Carolinas. And the wind was picking up.

## CHAPTER 16

# WHO'LL GIMME TWENTY?

WITH LESS THAN TWO HOURS left until I was done on the air for the year, after I broke for the news, my email popped with a note from Bruce Lawrence, Director of the Charlotte Make-A-Wish office. Subject: Panthers' Playoff Tickets for Hope.

The Panthers had made the playoffs. Actually, the Panthers had skidded into the playoffs. After starting the season with five straight wins – most of them frenzied finishes – the Cardiac Cats were steamrolled by the Tennessee Titans 37-17. With Hope Stout in the stands wearing the stinky gloves she'd been given before the game by Kevin Donnalley, the Panthers were pummeled from opening kick to final gun. The headline in the *Charlotte Observer* proclaimed "THUD." The team put a positive spin on the loss, or tried to, saying it was a wake-up call; something they needed, maybe. They'd been flying high those first five weeks, and this would bring them into the real world, get them ready to grind out the rest of the season.

A grind it was. They bounced back the next week to pull off another come-from-behind overtime win over New Orleans on a John Kasay field goal; but in Houston the following Sunday, managed to find a level of lame below even that of their Tennessee shellacking. The Panthers were 6-2 halfway through the season. Back in Charlotte to host the rematch with Tampa Bay, the Cats went cardiac again in front of more than 69,000 fans. Another come-from-behind, last-seconds, 27-24 win on what *Charlotte Observer* sports columnist Scott Fowler said was, "Flat out the best winning touchdown drive the Panthers have ever made." Protected by his Fat Cats, Jake Delhomme drove 78 yards in 95 seconds with no timeouts. The touchdown that would give the Super Bowl champs their second loss of the season at the hands of the Panthers came on a short pass to Steve Smith with only 1:06 left on the clock.

The next Sunday, November 16, the Panthers wouldn't cut it nearly so close. They pulled out a come-from-behind win, 20-17, over the Washington Redskins on a Stephen Davis touchdown run with a whole 1:09 left. More than 70,000 fans poured out of the stadium into the streets of uptown Charlotte with joy in their hearts and postseason in their sights. The Panthers were now 8-2 and needed only one more win to lock up a playoff berth for the first time in six years. No one saw the next three weeks coming.

November 23. Texas Stadium, Irving Texas. Dallas Cowboys. Panthers gave up ten points on turnovers, and their cardiac comeback was thwarted. Lost 24-20. Now 8-3.

November 30. Panther Stadium, Charlotte. Philadelphia Eagles. No magic in John Kasay's leg that day. One of the league's most consistent kickers missed his first point-after-touchdown in twelve years and also missed three field goals. Kasay muffed ten points, and the Panthers lost by nine, 25-16. Now 8-4.

December 7. Down Interstate 85 to the Georgia Dome. Rematch with Atlanta. This time the late fourth quarter comeback belonged to the Falcons, who sent the game into overtime on a Michael Vick touchdown run. The Panthers won the coin toss and got the ball first, but on their third play, Jake Delhomme threw right into the arms of Atlanta cornerback Kevin Mathis for an interception. Delhomme was the last Panther between Mathis and the end zone and blew the tackle. Touchdown. Lost 20-14. Now 8-5.

What the hell? The Panthers were 8-2 and a virtual lock as NFC South Division Champions after beating the Redskins. That was a month ago. They had now dropped three in a row, looked lousy in the losses, and slipped to 8-5. They'd gone from winning cardiac games on their way to a sure playoff spot to losing cardiac games on a path to watching the playoffs on TV. Once again, the Panthers needed not just a win, but to save their season.

Thank God for Arizona.

It was a perfect December 14 in the Valley of the Sun; a comfortable 63 degrees. Yet only 23,217 fans bothered to show up at Sun Devil Stadium, nestled between the buttes in Tempe. That's how out of it the Arizona Cardinals were. They were 3-10 and had been outscored by their opponents 387 to 180, yet the back-sliding Panthers barely beat them. John Kasay came through from 49 yards out with four seconds left in the game for a 20-17 win.

But a win is a win, and as ugly as it was, the Panthers not only clinched a playoff spot for the first time since 1996, but they cardiac'd themselves into first place in the NFC South Division. For the first time in seven seasons, there would be a playoff game in Charlotte.

"10:05 NOW. YESTERDAY, the final 8,000 seats went on sale and sold in less than forty minutes for the Panthers' playoff game. So unless you're a season ticket holder, or unless you were one of the 8,000 yesterday, if you want to be a part of history, go to that playoff game, it's over. It's done. You can't. There's no way. It's not possible."

(Shift to puzzled dumb-guy voice.) "Huh? Uhh... I wonder if Larson's got some tickets to auction off or somethin'?"

Grins from Bo and Mark.

"Got this from the Make-A-Wish people a little bit ago. 'Jon Richardson, son of owner Jerry Richardson, and the Carolina Panthers were listening to the show, and you talking about Hope, and have been moved to donate four VIP tickets to the first playoff game.' That'll be either Saturday, January 3 or Sunday, the fourth, depending on who they play."

"Now, listen up. Before you go to the wallet or the credit card or whatever, these tickets are to the Panthers' first playoff game since 1996. *Four ticket*s — so that makes it a party! Four *lower level* tickets to the game. Fifty-yard line. Right behind the Panthers' bench. Includes VIP parking and also four pre-game VIP field passes. This is not your average ticket deal.

"We don't have a lot of time, so I guess we're going to have to call this at noon, right? Because I'm done at noon for Christmas. So we're going to..."

Before I even said it officially, every phone line was flashing.

"...auction off these four tickets from the Panthers right now, right here in the studio. So, highest bidder. 704-570-11-10. Right now.

"Now where do I start the bidding? Bo and Mark and I were thinking this has to start at a grand, doesn't it? Got to start at a grand. Now, if you're one of the people who's got the phones lit up already and you can't do a thousand dollars, then thank you. God bless you. Please call the Make-A-Wish number or go to the websites and make a contribution to the Hope Stout fund directly. Everyone will really appreciate that. But I mean, four tickets straight from the Panthers. Choicest seats, parking, field passes, for the first Panthers' playoff game since '96."

I was on the air talking Panthers and playoffs and Hope and wishes while off air in the studio, chaos was breaking out.

"I'm not going to be able to take these calls on the air. I just can't do that. I'm going to talk with Stuart Stout here in a bit. Mark and Bo are taking the calls and are going to have Make-A-Wish verify the bids. I'll keep you posted on the bidding, but I'm no auctioneer..."

(Shift to twangy auctioneer voice.) *"Who'llgimmetwenty nowgimmetwentydollars.*

"Wait. Have we done the thousand dollars? I think we're hitting a verified thousand dollars this quickly."

Bo had his ears on the show and his eyes on Mark and shot two thumbs up letting out a big "OH YEAH!" to my thousand dollar inquiry. I kept running down all things Hope and wishes and Panthers and playoffs, and quickly, we were up to a couple thousand dollars. I was easing through emails and taking our breaks and talking playoffs and Hope and wishes and Panthers, and soon we were up to $5,000. It was a radio show doing itself, and an auction running itself, just as all that had been happening since Friday morning had been happening by itself – or because a 12-year-old girl with one-hundred-percent faith in God had wished it. It felt like we needed to take a breath and call timeout, but there wasn't time. In a blink it was 11:30 and I was into the news, and in a few moments more, my last half-hour. Before wrapping up the show for the year, I would talk wishes and Panthers and playoffs and Hope with Stuart Stout.

SEEMED LIKE THE LAST THING I had known I was heading off to work Friday morning with a solid sketch of that day's show, along with Monday's and Tuesday's, pretty well set in my mind. Some old friends to talk with, traditional

Christmas things to do, deal with whatever might be in the news those final few shows before the holidays, which typically isn't much. On Tuesday I'd have a few, no-doubt, *profound* thoughts just before noon, then give Bo the cue to roll John Lennon's "Happy Christmas" and exit stage left for a thirteen-day escape. I was now headed into the last half-hour Tuesday, and the show was as much on autopilot as if those final days had gone according to plan, except it was auto-piloting itself on an entirely different course than I'd charted.

I hadn't seen it coming. How could I have? I hadn't seen *her* coming. I had heard of her, but I hadn't heard about her wish. Hadn't even seen her before as far as I knew, let alone ever met her. Then I saw her picture in the paper and "met" her in Elizabeth Leland's story. When I talked with her dad, he said I should talk with her. Exactly what Mark was thinking earlier that morning. I was afraid, just as when Mark tried to suggest it, but Stuart said it live on the air, so what was I going to do? Say no? Next thing I knew, she was on the phone. I hadn't seen her coming, but she came along and grabbed me, and we were off. I didn't know where we were going, and I for sure didn't know how we were going to get there. Bo and Mark had always chided me about over-managing things, trying to be in control, trying to lay out not only where we were going, but how we were going to get there. I have routines, plans, and approaches to doing the show every morning. It is a highly-refined, smooth-as-silk, never-miss-a-mark, fully-autopilot…

Once, in Hawaii, Nancy and I had gone parasailing. We were nervous. The guys running the operation were hung-over, scruffy-faced, twenty-somethings and had heavy metal banging out of the speakers. They were driving this skiff wildly about a mile offshore. The water was choppy and the wind was whipping, and I was struggling in the harness of the parasail to get it set right and to digest the instructions from one of the hung-over, scruffy-faced, twenty-somethings standing with me on the deck. The sail finally started to open and catch the wind, and as it did, I was knocked around but kept holding on. My senses and sensibilities had me fighting all the way, death-gripping a railing and trying with all I had to stay on the boat. Suddenly, the guy giving me the final instructions, through the wind and the waves and the roar of the motor, shouted, "LET GO!"

In an instant, the struggle was over. The tension was gone. The buffeting of the wind ceased because I was up in it, lifted gently off the deck by the outstretched sails that had caught the breeze. They had me, the sails and the breeze, and they held me and carried me. It was a beautiful, magical, wonderfully wild ride. And all I did was let go.

Friday morning, December 19, 2003, a little girl appeared, and through the wind and the waves and the roar of the motor of my own life, whispered, "Let go."

"11:35. BO, DO YOU HAVE your thing there?" He nodded.

**"Go ahead."**

Bo hit the button and out came the resonant sound of a big tympani drum roll…

(Shift to Ed McMahon on Jerry Lewis telethon type voice.) **"Here's the current high bid for the Panthers' playoff tickets."**

Tympani roll climaxes into a crescendo and…

**"Fifteen thousand dollars."**

Silence.

Speechless.

Finally something incredibly enlightened came out.

**"Amazing."**

## CHAPTER 17

# ON THE ROCK

MARK HAD STUART STOUT on the phone. "Stuart, how're you doing?"

"Just fine, Keith; how are you doing this morning?"

"Doing really well. I appreciate you talking with us one more time before we're out of here for the holidays. Wanted to get an update on things and talk about some of what's going on."

"Great. Well, I just want to... I don't think there's any way we can thank you and the folks at WBT enough. And I would also like to thank Jon Richardson personally. I just heard about the tickets. That's fantastic."

Stuart said he was doing well, but his voice sounded different.

"It is, and it's what you'd expect from so many people in the Carolinas. Our thing has been to put a little radio wave into the story, but it's Hope's thought. It's her message. Our piece of this is very, very tiny. I appreciate your comment, but it's really about Hope's message of truth. The truth of what this is all supposed to be about – giving selflessly to others *first*. That's what people are connecting with. Stuart, I read what I think is the most recent message up on that CaringBridge website. Hope's been having some challenges the last couple of days?"

"Yeah, we're in a... we're in a little bit of a challenge right now."

Stuart's voice definitely sounded… thinner. Higher pitched, and less certain than Friday.

"I spoke with Hope just before I went on the air here, and she just wants everybody to continue to pray for her."

He coughed.

"She wants you to know how much she appreciates, uh... everything you all are doing... uh..."

He was talking faster, and his voice seemed to be getting shaky.

"We do... have a pretty difficult time right now."

Definitely shaky.

"But Hope is... with that indomitable spirit... is continuing to fight... and we just ask everybody out there to... you know... This is a time for miracles... and... uh..."

Quivering hard.

"We need one. And we ask everybody to continue to pray for her."

Stuart was holding himself together, but he was a different-sounding man than when we had spoken only four days earlier. An email that had been waiting for me when I fired up my computer that morning suddenly registered.

> From: dane....@
> Sent: Monday, December 22, 2003 11:16 PM
> Subject: something you should know about Hope Stout
>
> ---
>
> Keith,
>
> Hope Stout is not doing well. Many people are unaware of the seriousness of her cancer. This morning she

began to have difficulty breathing. Please do not read
this over the air. Thank you for all you've done.
Friend of Hope.

I knew Hope's situation was serious. Battling cancer,
obviously she was very sick. I had picked up on her having
to work for her breaths over the course of our conversation
Friday, but I had no idea when we talked the hell she'd already
been through or just how extremely sick she really was.

HOPE'S VP-16 HIGH had started to slip away shortly after the
weekend of the high school Homecoming, "The Great Mast
General Store Candy Raid," and her unforgettable day at the
Panther game. The Hail Mary round of chemo had given her
a surge in mobility and a retreat of her pain, but a couple of
weeks later, it was the pain that surged and the mobility that
surrendered. They gave her more VP-16 in late October, but
at home this time, in a more moderate pill form. This was in
consideration of the side effects, along with the horrifying
prospect for Hope of yet another week in the hospital.

The cancer surging through her, and in particular, the
once again expanding tumor in her right leg, continued its
remorseless drive to conquer, stealing what was left of her
liberty along its way. The pain soon rendered Hope unwilling
to leave the futon where she spent her days, other than for
trips to the bathroom. So confined and cut off from the rest
of life in the house, she finally fled the upstairs for a daytime
residence on an air mattress in the den. As the disease marched
on, eventually leaving her unable to get from air mattress to
bathroom, those trips were eliminated in favor of a bedside
facility and the relinquishing of all remaining independence in
the act. This was crushing. Even the balm of a mother's infinite

love is limited in its power to soothe a 12-year-old girl's loss of dignity.

There were good times along the way. Kevin Donnalley had called Hope as promised the week after they'd met. He gave her his cell number, and she began calling him after games. She would console him after those mounting Panther losses and celebrate after wins. He always took her calls.

Donnalley stopped by to see Hope whenever he could bearing cool gifts, like one of his game jerseys and a black fleece Panther jacket. On Halloween he hung around for a while. He was a monster lineman on the field, but in real life he was a father of three, so he was right at home watching *SpongeBob SquarePants* with Hope, and partaking of the bag of suckers he'd brought her. The Halloween visit in particular perked Hope up. She had been deeply depressed that day and had decided not to go Trick or Treating, but Kevin hanging around that afternoon lifted her spirits. She put on the thick black glasses, pocket protector, and "Nutty Professor" buck teeth she and Emily Rutherford had decided on. Off they went, going house to house as two nerds, goofy and free-spirited, cruising around in a golf cart tricked out with headlights, a stereo, SpongeBob decals, and a fuzzy purple steering wheel cover. Generous friends and relatives had chipped in to buy and customize it.

By Thanksgiving, Hope was in no shape to take the annual family holiday trip to Holden Beach, but she insisted they make the one-hour drive to Shelby's mom and dad's. Though she had to spend the day lying on an air mattress, it was still family, food, football, and fun as always. Back home, they kept their tradition of decorating the Christmas tree over Thanksgiving weekend. Reaching up from the mattress where she lay, Hope was able to hang ornaments on low branches. It was her year to put the angel on the tree, and she did – stretching up as far as she could, holding Stuart's right hand with her left, while he set the angel on top.

Make-A-Wish had come in November, but it was, at first, not at all a thrilling thought for Stuart.

"Hope is not going to die," Stuart said. "Make-A-Wish is for terminally ill kids. Tell them thanks, but no thanks."

Holly stepped in. She had been in a group called "Kids for Wish Kids" that raised money for wishes. It would turn out that one of the wishes she had helped raise money for would be her own sister's. Holly assured her father that Make-A-Wish was not strictly for kids who were going to die but for kids battling life-threatening illnesses.

"Dad, a lot of kids survive. A former Wish Kid talked to our student council earlier this year, and he was amazing. He had cancer when he was in his teens and is now 25 or so and is completely healed."

Stuart consented.

How many of life's brightest moments have come as a result of a well-meaning dad being overruled by a daughter?

In early December, Hope returned to the hospital but not for anymore Hail Mary chemotherapy. She went in for a week of radiation. Dr. McMahon had long ago explained that radiation held no prospect as a cure because Hope's cancer was too widespread. The intent now was strictly to shrink the tumor in her leg a little bit in an attempt to lessen the pain. It was during these radiation treatments that the morphine pump appeared. It helped, and the radiation helped. The fact was, though, there was no relieving Hope's pain completely. She was constantly uncomfortable, and it wore her down. Her hospital stays before always meant decorated rooms and visitors and parties and Pudge-smuggling. This time Hope wanted to be alone with her family.

Even in her misery, she was still Hope. She posted a sign on her hospital room door: "DO NOT DISTURB UNLESS YOU ALSO WANT TO BE HOSPITALIZED!" It was reminiscent of a poster on the door of her bedroom at home: "YOU ARE AT THE DOOR OF HOPE'S ROOM! PLEASE KNOCK AT THE DOOR. OR IF YOU HAVE CLASS, USE THE DOORBELL." (Yes, Hope had an actual doorbell for her bedroom.) "MY EMAIL ADDRESS IS HOPESTOUT@DONOTENTERMYROOM.COM."

Every measure was taken to minimize, or at least not worsen, Hope's agony. They took to wheeling her down to radiation in her hospital bed rather than transferring her to and from a gurney. She couldn't move herself, and lifting her – with unforgiving tumors pressing into her shoulders and chest, and her other leg and hip, in addition to the massively invaded right leg – proved sheer torture. When the treatments were completed, the radiologist knew there'd be no getting Hope in and out of a car, so he sent her home in an ambulance. A rented hospital bed was waiting when she arrived replacing the air mattress in the downstairs den. She now couldn't escape the pain even lying down. The hospital bed at least made what angled reclining she could manage a little less terrible, and the trapeze bar overhead allowed her to help when she did have to be moved.

Through the home chemo and the radiation, the constancy of the cancer and the persistence of the pain, in the 48 days between Halloween and Friday, December 19, Hope had become frighteningly weaker. She could not leave her bed. She didn't want to see or even talk with her friends. The change showed in the dry erase board calendar she kept in her room. She had always kept it current, but its last entries were from two months ago and announced plans for a Homecoming game, trip to Boone, and going to a Panther game. So Hope's reaction on the nineteenth when Shelby told her, "Dad's going on the Keith Larson show to talk about your wish," caught her mom by surprise.

"Why are they talking to him and not to me?"

She perked up. And sat up. Shelby saw that look-out-world trademark determination flash on Hope's face in an instant.

"Don't worry. Dad'll take care of it."

And he did.

In just the right moment, Stuart Stout made me the offer I had feared in a way I couldn't refuse. Of course when she got on the air, she was clear and strong, upbeat and insightful. Fueled by faith and doing nothing more than honestly opening her heart, she unleashed her look-out-world trademark determination through the 50,000 watts of WBT to the Carolinas and beyond (and thanks to the internet and many candles lighting each other exponentially, *way* beyond). No one listening could have guessed just by hearing her how dire her condition had become. Until that breathiness crept in.

The next day, Saturday the twentieth, she was equally amazing as a video production crew descended on the Stout home to get video for the Celebration of Hope, the fundraiser planned for January 16. A full-blown make-up session with a real Hollywood-type make-up woman got Hope ready for her close-up. Under bright lights and diffusion screens, Hope delivered for the camera like the movie star she'd always dreamed of becoming. If only there was an Academy Award for "Best Performance by a 12-year-old girl battling raging bone cancer."

That evening, Hope's breathing became labored. Seriously so. She was barely able to catch her breath and had difficulty speaking. Stuart and Shelby were startled and immediately called the home health care nurses. The woman who came rushing over was the nurse who'd seen Hope more than any other and had checked on her just a few days before. She gave her a quick examination. Then, as gently as such a thing can be done, she explained to Stuart and Shelby that their daughter's body was beginning to shut down.

"I just hope she makes it through Christmas," the nurse said.

That was the reality in the Stout household as Stuart was on the air with me in my final few minutes of the year. That was what he, Shelby, Holly, Austin, and of course Hope, had been living since 24 hours after I had talked with Hope the past Friday. That was why Molly Grantham hadn't been able to interview Hope for her story Monday. That was why Stuart was sounding different. On Saturday a nurse had told him she hoped his daughter would make it through Christmas. It was now almost noon, December 23.

"STUART, I WISH I COULD CONVEY to you accurately, in the proper and true spirit, all the phone calls we've taken and all the emails we've gotten... people praying for the best for Hope and for you guys."

"We absolutely feel it, and you know, it's a difficult position for us to be in as parents and for our family. But we also feel all the love and support that's coming from this community... and... it's just... it's... an overwhelming thing."

He sounded overwhelmed but held steady.

"But this is all about Hope. I mean, this is exactly what she's like, the way she's been the past twelve years. The fact that she made this request didn't surprise her mother or me a bit, and we're just continuing to... stand on The Rock, and hopefully, we'll get the miracle we're looking for. But Hope is... She just wanted to tell everybody... to keep praying for her."

"Stuart... Stout. I know for all of the love and energy there is behind Hope's wish and granting it, there is also her illness, your family's circumstance. This is so challenging and sad, and yet so beautiful and uplifting at the same time. It's an emotional explosion. I don't know how you guys keep plugging away."

"Well, I think you do. We've..."

He got stronger suddenly.

"We've got the utmost faith in God; that He's going to get us through this. And then, you know, you don't have to look very far around here at our house to see the inspiration. She's... uh..."

Then in an instant was shaky again.

"...she's an inspiration... and has been for many years to me."

He was talking fast and trying to hide it, but a father's unmistakable pride and breaking heart, broke Stuart Stout's voice unmistakably.

COMING BACK FROM THE BREAK after talking with Stuart, there were only a couple of minutes left before I would give Bo the last hand cue of the show and of the year. It felt like there was so much to say, and at the same time, like it had all been said.

"On the CaringBridge website you can leave your thoughts and wishes for Hope Stout, for her family, and also about her incredible wish for the other kids. An effort which, since the *Charlotte Observer* wrote about it and we've been talking about it and other people picked it up and are doing things, well, I don't have any way of knowing the exact current number, but an amazing amount of money has been received for granting those wishes in just the last few days. An amount of money the Make-A-Wish people said would normally have taken months.

"It speaks to the nature of Hope's message. The truth in it, the truth of giving of yourself for others, of loving others first, doing for others first — especially for the kids, especially at this time of year. The truth in that message, and its resonance with so many of you in your own hearts and in your own pocketbooks, is what has done it.

"If over the course of the next couple of minutes we get a bid above the $15,000 for the four Panthers tickets, I'll find a way to let you know before we actually slide into the news. Right now it's at fifteen grand, verified. Thank you so much to that apparent high bidder. Any other small or large contributions to Make-A-Wish, we appreciate.

"Just pray for Hope Stout and her family this holiday season, and for what she's trying to accomplish. I get to the end of each year, to Christmas, and think about the things we've done or things yet to do. That's the thought I go into each Christmas with. A lot of you have done something or are doing something this year to make a difference, so Merry Christmas."

At the snapping wave of my hand, Bo fired the button, and as quick as I'd said "Merry Christmas," thousands heard John Lennon.

"So this is Christmas, and what have you done?"

As they had for most of my final nine hours of radio for the year, the phone lines kept flashing, and the emails kept popping. John Lennon kept singing. But for the radio show, it was over. For us, it was now truly in God's hands and in the hands of others. I'd never experienced anything like the 96 hours since Hope Stout cracked my heart in the most beautiful way: "Thank you for having me on the show. It's a big honor!" I felt like we had done what we could and knew we had done a lot. But for some reason, in that moment, it felt like a fragment of a sentence had been left dangling, its thought unfinished, no punctuation at the end.

My microphone was off and wouldn't be turned on again until just after nine o'clock Monday morning, January 5, 2004.

But then it was.

As John and Yoko and the kids in the choir were singing their final chorus, **"Let's hope it's a good one, without any fear,"** Mark rushed over with a confirmation from the Make-A-Wish people we'd been desperately hoping for. Bo scrambled to the controls to punch my mic back on a split-second before the noon news sounder.

**"We just bagged an elephant!"**

# CHAPTER 18

# SILENT NIGHT

WEDNESDAY MORNING, CHRISTMAS EVE. The picture of the smiling, pondering, pensive Hope Stout in her jade-green bandana, gazing into the eyes of the tiny gray kitten she was pulling up close to her face, leapt from the *Charlotte Observer* once again.

### RUSH TO MAKE WISH COME TRUE
### MONEY POURS IN AS YOUNG
### GIRL FALLS GRAVELY ILL
#### Man gives $100,000; a family skips
#### Disney trip, donates $5,000

As irrelevant as newspapers supposedly are in the age of the internet and 24-hour TV news, seeing the words *"Girl Falls Gravely Ill"* in unforgiving black ink on pale newsprint, packed a hell of a punch.

As a 12-year-old girl with bone cancer fell gravely ill this week, people in the Carolinas rushed to help make her wish come true.

One man brought a certified check for $100,000 to the Make-A-Wish Foundation on Tuesday. He asked to remain anonymous.

He hadn't been anonymous to me.

His name was Jeff Fowlkes, and he wasn't the kind of elephant we'd been thinking of. He wasn't one of Charlotte's banking giants, NASCAR stars, or textile or tobacco titans. He wasn't one of the moneyed moguls the Carolinas had come to rely on to write a fat check to bail out a charity in a desperate bind, or make some civic project happen. He was the head of a small local company that put on cheerleading competitions throughout the Southeast.

He had first emailed me on Monday shortly after the show. He told me a little about his company and said he wanted to meet to discuss Hope Stout. He said he was a regular listener; he said, "We may be in a position to do something BIG here." He said he was reaching out because he had been touched by my words. He gave me multiple phone numbers and asked me to give him a call.

I didn't, but I did email him early Tuesday morning to apologize and told him I would try to call that afternoon. His reply came midway through my show. He said he certainly understood and graciously thanked me for what I had done for Hope. He also said, "We are making a contribution today."

It never clicked.

Late in the show we had gotten word from the Make-A-Wish people that a big donation might be happening, but they didn't want to say anything until it was verified. We were hoping like crazy it was true, but we were consumed with auctioning Panthers' playoff tickets, talking with Stuart Stout, and getting ready to wrap up for the year. I desperately wanted to make the announcement before signing off but couldn't even hint at it. Before I knew it, John and Yoko and the children were singing. As the song was fading, Mark got the call from Make-A-Wish: CONFIRMED! A certified check for $100,000 was being delivered to the foundation's office.

"Can I go with that?"

"Yep!"

"Bo?"

"Got it."

The tune had actually ended, and the clip from the big-voiced announcer-guy, **"This is the Keith Larson Show,"** was signing me off. The show was over but Bo cut me in live.

**"GO!"**

Only enough time for five words about an elephant.

ALONG WITH MOST OF THE CAROLINAS, I was downshifting into Christmas vacation gear as Wednesday wore on, but Molly Grantham was just gearing up. Over the next several days, the *Charlotte Observer* continued with updates, and other TV stations did stories too, but no one did more to keep Hope Stout on the minds of people in the Carolinas over the holidays than WBTV's Molly Grantham. She told story after story about Hope and her wish.

She kept up with the fundraising:

**"People from all around the country are signing the guestbook on Hope Stout's CaringBridge website; checks of every amount are pouring in."**

Girl about Hope's age who made donation (video clip): **"She's just a normal 12-year-old girl, but she's doing something really, really great."**

**"The people at Make-A-Wish say any amount helps. Checks for thirty, fifty, one hundred dollars line the table. The phones go crazy. People are walking in as we're interviewing."** (Video clip showing that actually happening.)

Chuck Coira from Make-A-Wish (video clip): **"Hope's father, Stuart, told me the only thing that could save Hope at this point was a miracle.**

"But maybe, the miracle is what we're already witnessing." (Video clip of piles of checks.) "They are up to $370,000."

She kept up with Hope:

"Hope had a good day. She was upstairs playing video games with her sisters."

Shelby Stout (video clip): "There's no more medicine we're going to do. It's more for pain relief right now. We have always put it in God's hands."

And Molly was the first to catch up with Hope's Panther, Kevin Donnalley:

"When you see him after the game on the sideline talking on his cell phone, he just may be talking with 12-year-old Hope Stout."

Donnalley (video clip): "I remember getting back to Charlotte. Your cell phones are off during the flight, so I flipped it on, and there was a message waiting. It was Hope! And she says, 'I wanted to make sure you got back to Charlotte okay. You guys played a tough game.'"

"Donnalley says that one call says it all. Hope is unselfish, sensitive, and wise beyond her years. In fact, Kevin says he once asked Hope if he could do anything to help."

Donnalley (video clip): "She said, 'You know what, I have a great family. They're really supportive of me. So if you or your teammates could go over to the hospital, see some of those kids over there... There's a lot of kids that don't have family... brothers or sisters... so if you could, go over there and visit them instead of coming to see me all the time.' And my jaw dropped."

Grantham brought stories of people being swept up by Hope into living rooms across the Carolinas. All kinds of people, especially children:

"Six-year-old Olivia Roussey is giving up her allowance."

Olivia (video clip): "I went up to my room and got three dollars, and I put it in a piece of paper with a note." (Clip showing note in child's handwriting: "Dear Hope, I am giving you $3. I hope that is enough for you. Love, Olivia.")

"Her 8-year-old sister, Jessica, is doing the same."

Jessica (video clip): "I gave her thirteen dollars."

"They say, Hope's desire to help other kids, is *'cool.'*"

"We just got an updated total. Make-A-Wish is now up to $447,000."

And she told of people sweeping up Hope and her family:

"On Christmas Eve, the Stout family heard a knock on their door. When they opened it, dozens upon dozens of people were filling up their entire front yard holding candles, singing, and praying for their daughter. The Stouts say *that's* what it is truly all about."

There had, in fact, been about 150 people singing "Silent Night" in front of the Stouts' home in the cool, dark stillness of Christmas Eve. Emily Rutherford was there along with her mom and Aunt Tamara – the conspiring sisters – and also Gina Wheeling and her parents. There were friends who had prepared meals during Hope's long ordeal, had decorated her hospital room, or held the Stouts' hands at church. Kevin Donnalley was there with his wife and kids. I was there with mine.

# CHAPTER 19

# KEEP POUNDING

THE MORNING OF NEW YEAR'S EVE, *Charlotte Observer* columnist Don Hudson jumped in.

## PANTHER CAN'T WAIT FOR THIS DATE
### Donnalley joins "Celebration of Hope"

Kevin Donnalley has the biggest date of his life coming up. The Carolina Panthers' right guard and 1990 University of North Carolina alumnus will suit up in prime-time, a co-star in a miracle story.

But it isn't what you think.

It's bigger than the Panthers' playoff game Saturday with the Dallas Cowboys. And in this town, this week, that's big.

On January 16, Donnalley plans to put on a tuxedo and escort Hope Stout from her limousine into the spotlights at the Celebration of Hope party at the Charlotte Westin.

"The playoffs are huge," Donnalley said Tuesday. "But this little girl has done so much to help these kids through Make-A-Wish."

Playoff fever was running high in Charlotte. The wild card slot against the Panthers had been locked up by the Dallas Cowboys. Their well had run dry with 5-11 records the past three years, but in 2003, the Cowboys hired former New York Giants and New England Patriots head coach, Bill Parcells. He immediately orchestrated a turnaround to 10-6 and got Dallas into the playoffs for the first time since 1999. The Cowboys looked like they were on their way to becoming "America's Team" once again, and a prime-time playoff game against them was the biggest thing in Charlotte in years.

Don Hudson was right. The game wasn't any bigger than the hold a little girl battling cancer had on the city. The stories of the girl, her wish, and the Panthers had, in fact, been weaving themselves into one. Carolinians learned what a Panther fan Hope had been and of her support for the cancer-battling Mark Fields and Sam Mills. She had come into Mark and Jon Richardson's orbit and pulled them into hers. They had shown their support of Hope and her wish in many ways, including the playoff tickets that brought a fast $15,000. Molly Grantham showed Hope at the Tennessee game and Kevin Donnalley talking about his relationship with her. Don Hudson ran a picture of the senior Fat Cat and the little girl together in their Panther jerseys and told of Donnalley's plan to be Hope's date for the big bash she had planned to cap off the million-dollar fundraising drive.

Hope chose January 16 for the dinner, two nights before the NFC Championship Game. That's so Donnalley could attend if the team is still playing. The odds say it won't be.

174

SATURDAY, JANUARY 3, 2003. The day – the night – of the Carolina Panthers' first home playoff game since 1996. For those lucky enough, or moneyed enough, to have tickets, the tailgating around the stadium started late morning. It was an incredible carnival atmosphere. Around the city, the backyard parties started midafternoon, with grills and smokers turning out burgers and barbecue – Carolina style. Sports bars and restaurants with TVs were packed by happy hour. Panther Stadium was bursting with 72,324 fans. Deep inside, John Fox set the stage.

"I told you early on I like this football team, and I still like this football team. And you need to think BIG.

"We're going to whip these guys, and we're gonna go to St. Louis, and we're gonna whip them. And we're going to come back, and we're gonna play Green Bay here. But we've got to take care of business *tonight*.

"A lot's been made of our opponent, but this is our time. Expect to play great tonight."

In a locker room packed with big, boisterous men whose hearts were pumping with adrenaline, a smaller, quiet man rose to speak. He wasn't wearing a jersey, but his number 51 was underneath every one of theirs.

Sam Mills was only 5-foot-9, but he stood like a giant in front of the Panthers. He'd been told in August that he only had a few months to live. He'd gone through four months of chemotherapy and radiation, rarely missing a day of work as linebackers coach, and he had never uttered a word about his ordeal – until now.

Mills told his teammates that when he was diagnosed, there were two things that could have happened.

"I could have quit and given up. Or I could fight. I only knew one way, and that was to fight. You need to make the same choice. Go out there and fight, guys. Keep pounding.

Keep pounding. Keep pounding. No matter what it looks like, keep pounding."

PANTHER FANS, who weren't at the game but were in front of televisions, were in good company. It was prime-time, coast to coast, Saturday night playoff football. The Carolina Panthers – whom the national sports media was calling the Cinderella team of the season – were hosting the Dallas Cowboys, one of the NFL's biggest TV draws, on ABC. The superstar broadcast team of Al Michaels and John Madden were in the booth. Many millions around the country were watching shortly after the start of the game when Michaels tossed to sideline reporter Lisa Guerrero:

"Panther right guard Kevin Donnalley was very much looking forward to the spotlight of tonight's game. Not for himself, not for his teammates, but for a 12-year-old girl by the name of Hope Stout. He met her earlier this season." (Picture of Hope and Donnalley meeting at the Panther game and other photos of Hope were shown.) "She's been battling a rare form of bone cancer and has become an inspiration to him. Here's an example of her selflessness. When the Make-A-Wish Foundation asked her what she would like granted, she said she wanted the wishes granted of the other 155 children battling life-threatening illnesses in this region. The cost: about $1,000,000. Donnalley wants to help her raise it. So far, they've raised about $400,000. For information on how you can help, you can contact the Carolina Panthers."

Kevin Donnalley and the Carolina Panthers pounded the Dallas Cowboys exactly as Sam Mills had challenged them. They played with Hope in their hearts, just as Donnalley had "Hope" written on his gloves. They held the same Cowboys, who had beaten them 24-20 six weeks earlier, to only ten points. The Panthers scored 29. They expected to play great, they *did* play great, and they were on to St. Louis for the divisional round of the playoffs against the Rams.

The Stouts were caught up in playoff mania, of course. Holly and Austin used the family tickets and were at the game; Stuart and Shelby were at home with Hope. They were watching in the den when Lisa Guerrero told the world about their daughter, who lay in her nearby hospital bed, drifting in and out of sleep. When they saw Hope in her Panther jersey with Kevin Donnalley flash onto their screen, just as she was flashing across millions of other TV screens, they jumped from their seats.

"Hope! There you are – *there you are*! You're on national TV!"

Stuart ran over to the bed. "Hopie, you are famous!" he said, confirming the wish she hadn't made for herself had come true anyway because of the wish she had instead made for others. She died the next day.

# CHAPTER 20

# THERE'S ALWAYS HOPE

MONDAY MORNING, JANUARY 5, 2004, the photo of the smiling, pondering, pensive Hope Stout in her jade-green bandana, gazing into the eyes of the tiny gray kitten she was pulling up close to her face, returned once again to the *Charlotte Observer*. It leapt from the front page more mesmerizing than ever, above the fold, under the headline of Don Hudson's story:

### DEATH STRENGTHENS DESIRE TO GRANT HOPE'S LAST WISH
*Celebration She Planned Will Go On*

Hope Stout, Charlotte's miracle child of 2003, died Sunday evening.…

Unlike Hope's first appearance on the front page seventeen days earlier, I saw this one the moment I grabbed my paper, in the cool darkness of 5:29 in the morning, as I fired up my highly-refined, smooth-as-silk, never-miss-a-mark, fully-autopilot drive to work and show-prep routine for the first time in almost two weeks. That morning, unlike Friday, December 19, I knew I would see Hope on the front page. I had gotten a call at home Sunday from Chuck Coira shortly after Hope passed away. I was stunned but not surprised.

I had been trading occasional emails with Stuart since he sent me that first one a few hours after Hope had been on the show. On December 29, he told me he didn't see how Hope could make it much longer. She was getting very weak and was sleeping a lot, he said, but when she was awake, she was alert and very much aware of what was going on.

On New Year's Eve, I wrote to tell him how excited I was about Don Hudson's column that morning about Hope and Kevin Donnalley. Hudson was the *Observer's* highest-profile columnist and was sometimes a target of mine on the show, but I had emailed, telling him what a great column it was about Hope and Donnalley. I said I'd be sure to give him the credit he deserved when I got back on the air. I was beginning to make some early plans for the first show after vacation when I emailed Stuart on December 31:

"…I'm back on the air this Monday, and I wonder if we could get you on for a few minutes – follow up, revitalize the fundraising effort? If that's basically okay let me know, and I'll have Mark get in touch with you Monday morning to set a specific time. Thanks. All prayers and good thoughts continue."

"…You got it. Call me on my cell phone Monday. She is still hanging in there as of this morning. Her mom asked her yesterday if she thought she was dying and she said, 'Gee Mom, I don't know. I've never done that before!'"

Shelby had no doubt Hope was dying when death came Sunday night.

That morning Hope had started moaning. A low, occasional, sometimes rhythmic moan. It was disturbing. They had nurses in to check on her. They replenished and increased her morphine drip and assured everyone she was not in pain.

The moaning, the nurses explained, was Hope's body pushing air out of her lungs. Her cancer-riddled, chemo-beaten body was preparing to let her go.

Throughout the day they all stayed close, save for the few minutes Stuart ran out to pick up some chicken to throw on the grill. They had to eat, and the unimaginably unreal nature of what was happening in their den somehow made Stuart gravitate to something entirely real. For the Stout family, Stuart at the grill on Sunday was about as real as it got. With Hope just a few steps away in her hospital bed, Shelby, Austin, and Holly joined Stuart in the kitchen as he brought in the steaming platter of chicken. No one could eat a bite.

Not long after, Shelby was at her post at the side of the bed when suddenly the moaning stopped. Hope's breathing slowed. Shelby knew. She yelled for Stuart, who was out closing up the grill. He came running. As he joined his wife at Hope's bedside, what struck Stuart, even in his horror at what was happening, was Hope's peacefulness. She wasn't suffering. They each held one of her hands as Holly and Austin came close.

"We love you Hope!"

A few more breaths.

"Daddy loves you, baby!"

Each more shallow than the one before.

"Run to Jesus, Hope!"

She exhaled softly into stillness, smiling.

HOPE'S DEATH was on the front page of the *Observer* on Monday morning, all over WBT and many other radio stations, and on all the Charlotte TV stations – especially WBTV. Molly Grantham, in black, would lead the newscasts that night. The news was everywhere, and it had Charlotte awakening to a hurt in its heart. When there's a celebration, everyone celebrates; when there's a hurt, everyone hurts.

But it wasn't only Charlotte, and not even just the Carolinas anymore. The story of the 12-year-old North Carolina girl who was battling bone cancer and had used her chance to "Make-A-Wish" to make one for others, had been, in the last few days, getting picked up by news wires, websites, and bloggers and was rapidly rippling around the country. In fact, around the world.

The *Atlanta Journal Constitution*, *Newsday*, *Duluth Minnesota Tribune*, *Sarasota Herald-Tribune*, and the *Guardian* in London – *England* – were just some among the scores of papers and magazines carrying the story. Dozens of TV stations did too, along with widely read websites like *World Net Daily*, which had run lengthy stories about Hope and her wish. And don't believe the reputation Dallas has of not caring about what goes on outside the Lone Star State. When the *Dallas Morning News* ran the story that the little girl Cowboys' fans had seen during the playoff game had died, phones in the Dallas Make-A-Wish office rang with donations.

Just after 9 a.m., Bo opened my first show back from vacation with a montage from Friday, December 19, featuring the clear, bright, optimistic, young voice of Hope Stout.

**"To have these kids' wishes come true... I know we can do it."**

**"Just have one-hundred-percent faith in God. Anything can happen."**

**"Thank you for having me on the show. It's a big honor!"**

Bo was zoned into the mechanics of running the board, but Mark was listening. Hearing Hope again against the news of the morning had him choking it back in seconds. I listened closely to the whole piece too. This time, somehow, I was calm and clear.

"That's Hope Stout from when we talked with her Friday, December 19. Cancer won its battle with Hope's body last night, but it had already lost its battle with her spirit. Hope lives. Hope and her family have faith. Hope and her family, through their faith, have love. And with that kind of love, there's always hope. Always.

"Bo, Mark... good morning.

"I guess it's not a real big secret that I have found myself, the last few weeks, affected by this spunky little kid; infected by her since we talked with her. Somehow, hearing her talk about her own sickness, hearing her talk about her own wish, hearing her explain it herself – she and her family and that wish of hers haven't seemed to leave my brain for very long. A lot of you feel the same way. I feel... just by having been available, having been used as something of a channel for her... I feel, we all do in here, compelled to see this wish through. Frankly, I know that's going to happen. What's gone on the past couple of weeks has been amazing.

"Back when we read Elizabeth Leland's story in the *Observer* and started talking about it... and the Make-A-Wish people saying it would take a million bucks... we said, *Hey, wouldn't it be great if we could raise that money by Christmas, so these kids could know their wishes would be granted as Christmas presents?* That was not even a stretch goal kind of thought..."

It was a crazy thought.

"But by noon the following Tuesday, the Carolinas had responded with more than a quarter of a million dollars. In the week and a half since, another quarter million has been raised; $500,000 so far. And who was the real star of the Panther game Saturday night?! So I have no doubt the million will be raised by the Celebration of Hope next week. It's happening.

"Hope had a childlike wish to be on a TV show, be a TV star. But when the Make-A-Wish people came, her first thought was not about that TV show-TV star thing. It was for the other kids... that their wishes would be granted. She said this is what God had placed in her heart... to worry about the others first... to care for the others first, and selflessly, she did that, and wished her wish, and it has commenced. It has been undertaken and taken up by so many of you. In doing that, Hope, it turns out, became a star herself. To the point that on Saturday night, as no doubt tens of millions of Americans tuned in to the Panther-Dallas game, they saw the face and the smile and the *hope* of Hope Stout, thanks to Kevin Donnalley and ABC. Hope became a full-fledged TV star. So it *did* happen, but it happened by putting others first. I've read somewhere, that's what we're supposed to do."

That day I did some typical first-day-back-after-the-holidays stuff, like thwacking several local politicians for their cheesy holiday cards and mocking predictable New Year's resolutions. Mostly though, I talked about Hope and her wish and the Panthers.

Without mentioning his name, I talked about the elephant that had been bagged that last Tuesday before Christmas; how he wasn't really what we would think of as a rich elephant at all. He was a regular guy with a family of his own, who said he'd been deeply moved when he had heard Hope.

We got a fundraising update from Chuck Coira, who told more stories of kids and families giving of themselves, giving what they could, giving up Christmas presents to make Hope's wish come true. He said some of the kids on the list were beginning to have their wishes actually come true – trips to Disneyland; ponies – because of the money pouring in. A 5-year-old girl's wish was to see the grandmother she'd never seen because Grandma lived in Panama. Make-A-Wish had flown Grandma in for Christmas.

I talked about the Christmas Eve gathering at the Stouts, about Molly Grantham's stories and other coverage I'd seen or heard or knew of. I told of stories about Hope that were turning up all around the country and the world. I made sure to give Don Hudson unqualified credit for terrific columns, as promised. What I did not do was the one thing I had specifically been planning to do my first day back – talk with Stuart Stout. He may have been willing, but I couldn't ask. What I *did* do was read what Stuart had posted on Hope's CaringBridge website journal at 9:14 the night before:

> Hello, to all. It is Sunday night and heaven has a new angel. Hope's courageous battle ended tonight very peacefully at 8:30. She was surrounded by her family and her precious cats. We thank God for allowing Hope to be our daughter. It was the greatest gift Shelby and I could ever have.
>
> We love all of you and continue to ask for your prayers for our family.
>
> 'For those who hope in the Lord will renew their strength. They will soar on wings like eagles; run and not grow weary; they will walk and not be faint.'
>
> In His name, Stuart.

Later that morning, I spoke for the first time with Hope's Panther Kevin Donnalley, after Bo replayed the Lisa Guerrero story.

"What an amazing moment that was Saturday night in the Panther game. And on the phone with us now is Carolina Panthers' big number 65, right guard Kevin Donnalley. Hello Kevin."

"Hi. How're you doing today?"

"I'm doing very well. Welcome to WBT. It's good to talk with you. From what we've heard, you had a lot to do with making that story about Hope happen on ABC Saturday night. Were you aware they had done it, or were going to do it?"

"I didn't know for sure. Earlier in the week, Make-A-Wish called and we brainstormed ideas. I got back to the stadium and was talking with anybody who'd listen to me. Charlie Dayton, our media relations guy, he had a lot to do with it. We tried to convince Lisa Guerrero. I was just glad she went with it."

"It was terrific they were able to do it, and especially early in the game, knowing what Hope's wish would have been, to be a TV star, and to have that on the game Saturday. It's great you were able to make it happen."

"I'd go visit her and we would talk about different things, and sometimes, the TV would be on. We'd be watching Nickelodeon or the Disney Channel and we'd see a show like *Lizzy McGuire* or *That's So Raven*. I have an 8-year-old girl who likes to watch them also, and Hope said she'd like to be on one of those shows. It was something that would have been very special to her, and she probably could have had that wish granted, but she gave it up and wanted to do it for all the other kids. Getting to know her the past six or eight weeks, it didn't surprise me at all when I heard that was her wish. I was blown away by it, but at the same time it was like, *That's Hope!*"

"I love the picture they printed in the *Observer* of you with Hope before the Tennessee game. She's beaming."

"She was always happy. I just wish I could put into words what kind of person she was, but by her actions, you can tell. And you know, I'm kind of focused before games, and I don't like to have a lot of distractions. I saw her, and the first thing that hit me was the red hair because I have a middle child that has red hair. It's like they have the same personality. She was just so full of life and like her name... Hope. There's so many bad things going on in this world... horrible things and news stories... and just one story like this can make you have faith in mankind again."

"Kevin, the Celebration of Hope is coming up on the sixteenth, and I know it was your plan to escort Hope to the event. Are you still going to be there?"

"Yes. It's a Friday night, and that would be the weekend of the NFC Championship, but I don't see any way I could miss that event. I'm going to invite some of my buddies from the team. It's going to be a great night. We can take care of business this weekend in St. Louis and then, well, I think Charlotte really deserves something here, because this team has been through a lot the last few years. To have such a special group of guys like we have this year and knowing how hard we've worked... it's fun, and I'm glad to see it for the fans."

"Kevin, I'm not above connecting the dots. Come on out. Buy a couple of tickets for the Celebration of Hope. You'll be doing something you'll feel great about when you help Make-A-Wish grant these wishes for Hope Stout, for the other 155 kids, and you'll be there that Friday night and see Kevin Donnalley and some of the other Panthers the weekend they will become the NFC Champions!"

"Yes!"

# CHAPTER 21

# PAGE 5-B

ON TUESDAY, the ramp-up began toward the Panthers' second-round playoff game against the Rams in St. Louis on Saturday night. Charter flights and ticket packages sold out fast. WBT launched a giveaway of a trip to St. Louis, including game tickets. Panther fans were eating it up, and non-fans were quickly jumping on the bandwagon. Blue and silver and black were being flown and worn all over town. Hope Stout was in the paper again, and I was on the air.

"Her middle name is Elizabeth. I didn't know that. Says so on page 5-B of the *Observer* today. Hope Elizabeth Stout. We never hear people's middle names unless they're charged with a crime. Until their story is on page 5-B.

"Cancer won its battle with Hope's body Sunday night, but it couldn't keep her spirit from healing the hearts of countless others, as people around the Carolinas and around the country contribute to give life to Hope's wish.

"I think this is the first time I've seen a photo of her in the paper without her bandana. Today's is a *before* picture. Looks like a typical school picture that should appear in a school yearbook. Not on page 5-B. No kid's picture should have to appear on page 5-B, whether because of a vicious illness or youthful decisions in automobiles.

"Page 5-B says the service for Hope Stout is tomorrow afternoon, two o'clock, Matthews United Methodist Church."

It wasn't just the *Charlotte Observer* Hope Stout appeared in that morning. Upwards of 200 newspapers, TV stations, and websites were carrying her story from Honolulu to upstate New York, from Green Bay, Wisconsin, to Riverside, California.

And CNN.

WEDNESDAY MORNING IT WAS NOT Hope Stout whose picture leapt from the front page above the fold of the *Charlotte Observer*. It was 6-year-old Adam Edwards of nearby Huntersville, and the smooth, shiny, bald head reaching out of his dark turtleneck told starkly Adam's unmistakable story. Yet his eyes sparkled as his mother braced him for a hug, and a stretching smile dimpled his cheeks. Adam Edwards was filled with joy – and clearly, so was his mom – because he was going to LEGOLAND – thanks to Hope Stout, whose funeral was that afternoon.

### *Sick Children Are Smiling Now*
## HOPE'S WISH:
## BIG DREAMS COME TRUE

*Kids' Wishes Granted by a 12-year-old's
Request*

By Don Hudson

Unlike other first-graders, Adam Edwards can't attend classes. He gets chemotherapy treatments every three weeks and is too sick for school. Plus, he can't risk catching germs from classmates.

But because of Hope Stout, 6-year-old Adam has something to look forward to. He will go to LEGOLAND near San Diego this summer.

This was exactly the story Charlotte needed to read on the day it would say goodbye to Hope.

Sammy Pelzer, 6, and his little sister Sarah, 5, of Newton, were diagnosed with familial dysautonomia three years ago. On Christmas weekend, Make-A-Wish paid $1,000 to ship them a pony named 'Thank Heaven' donated by a couple in Michigan whose daughter had outgrown it.

"I have not seen a more excited face on him in a long time," said Sammy's mother, a physician who gave up her practice to care for her two youngest children.

"It helped Sammy find a pony. Her wish has touched so many children."

Amber Ashworth, fifteen, of Ellerbe has osteosarcoma, the same disease that took Hope's life. For her wish, Amber and her family were flown to Miami on December 22 and boarded a ship for a five-day, expenses-paid cruise to the Bahamas.

Because of the aggressive nature of the cancer, Amber's cruise was considered a 'rush' wish. Hope's wish paid for it.

On December 20, Jamal Richmond, a 17-year-old Independence High School student who has Hodgkin's disease, was granted a $1,500 shopping spree. Jamal had the use of a limousine for his shopping day, as well as dinner with family and friends at Red Lobster.

A lot of children are still waiting. Cooper Lentz, a 3-year-old from New London, has clear cell sarcoma and wants to go to Walt Disney World.

But now they have Hope on their side, a redheaded angel who started taking care of them even before she left this world for the next.

∽⚭∾

WE THOUGHT WE SHOULD get to the church early. Neither Nancy nor I had been there before and didn't know how big it was. We figured a lot of people would be going.

Turns out, Matthews United Methodist is a very big church, and as we arrived around one for the two o'clock service, crowds were streaming in. The expansive parking lots were packed; police cruisers dotted the entrances, and officers directed traffic. TV news trucks from all of the Charlotte stations were parked out front with their tall relay masts rising above. Reporters and cameramen milled around.

Inside, people were already standing in the vestibule, and ushers were setting up chairs for the overflow. The balcony and choir loft would soon be packed, along with the stairs up to them. There were still a few scattered seats in the sanctuary; somebody waved us into a row in the middle that had room for two more.

Front and center of the church, on an easel placed only a few feet beyond the steps where she had once fought for her place alongside her new pastor, was a framed, blown-up photo of Hope. It was her sixth-grade picture. The last official school picture that would ever be taken of her – red hair radiating, smile beaming, a glint in the eye entirely revealing. Reverend Ken Lyon would say later, in that picture, Hope looked like she had just dumped a bowl of spaghetti on someone's head and gotten away with it. He was right. A 12-year-old girl's picture did not belong as the centerpiece of memorial service. It was also a picture that did not belong with a story on page 5-B of the paper.

The prelude music stopped, and a sudden silence swept through the church. The oxygen seemed sucked out of the room as close to 3,000 people simultaneously inhaled. The sound of a tense rustling rose as everyone turned, unprompted but on cue, toward the back of the church. Heartache hung in the air as nearly 6,000 eyes fixed on Stuart Stout, standing with the remaining three of his FOURCHIX, his arms wrapped around daughters Austin and Holly, with Shelby at Austin's side, their arms locked together. An emotional explosion was pending, needing only the slightest spark from the Stouts to set it off.

They could have. Grief and tears had been pouring from Stuart and his girls all day, right up through the limousine ride to the church. Then, as they arrived to the overwhelming outpouring of love evidenced by the countless cars; as they saw the oldest of old friends, some who had driven hours to be there; as they shared private moments with Pastor Ken in his study just before the service; as they stepped into the doorway of the sanctuary and the music took its pause to invite them to enter; and as they saw the photo taken of their beautiful daughter before cancer had invaded her body and their lives – they were filled with Hope once again.

Peace came to the Stouts as they took their seats walking past pews packed with family, friends, a big football player, a radio guy, and people they'd never even met.

THURSDAY MORNING it was Shelby Stout whose picture leapt from the *Charlotte Observer*. She was on the receiving end of a huge hug from a well-wisher at the reception that followed Hope's service. Her face was barely visible over the shoulder of the woman doing the hugging, but was enough so as to see her eyes, closed in heartache and relief all at once. Stuart looked on with care and love and loss but with a hint of serenity as well. Their daughter was gone and their hurt would never heal, but in their faith, they knew perfect healing had come to her.

## *Service Honors Hope's Life;*
## *Her Message Lives On*

By Don Hudson

Stuart Stout slowly made his way to the lectern at Matthews United Methodist Church on Wednesday afternoon, taking those heavy steps no father wants to take. But even in a moment of searing grief, he was able to smile and share a special piece of his extraordinary daughter.

"I'm sure within twenty minutes of arriving in heaven," Stuart said, "Hope looked around and told God, 'This is wonderful. This is really as I pictured it would be. But I have a few suggestions.'"

Wednesday's memorial service for Hope Stout was filled with laughter and tears.

The 12-year-old Weddington girl who inspired the city with her selflessness was eulogized before a packed church as a line of TV trucks outside waited to beam her story around the community and to the nation, where her message has inspired so many. There was an original song, and the preacher told how Hope's dream was to be a TV or movie star. He told how she created a TV show, called "Hoprah," where she was the host and played all the characters.

But the most moving tribute was a slide show documenting Hope's life, a short life where the one constant was a 110-watt smile that dominated every picture.

The song that accompanied the slide show was "Legacy" by Nicole Nordeman:

> I want to leave a legacy
> How will they remember me?
> Did I choose to love? Did I point to You enough
> to make a mark on things?
> I want to leave an offering
> A child of mercy and grace who
> blessed your name unapologetically
> And leave that kind of legacy

There were no dry eyes, but the tears rolled down over smiles.

FINALLY, FRIDAY.

"Hope Stout, whose spirit has proven to reach far beyond the mere bonds of life, was laid to rest Thursday morning. Private ceremony... cemetery near the family's home."

It felt odd somehow, Hope and her wish as part of "My News and You are Welcome to It," the riff on the news that opens the show. But I take that "week that was" slant at the end of each week, and Hope and her wish and the Panthers were the biggest news in the Carolinas.

"I'm told one of the TV stations reported last night that there were dozens at the memorial service for Hope Stout yesterday. I guess you could put it that way, that there were dozens. There were several *hundred* dozens.

"Stuart and Shelby Stout stood smiling and crying in the receiving line for more than two hours by the time I saw them. And I wasn't anywhere near the end.

"It is still amazing to me how unspeakably crushing and horrible, and indescribably beautiful and uplifting, can exist at the same time in minds and hearts and lives about a story... a person. It causes a massive explosion in the brain and heart.

"Now, we're moving into a big football weekend, a big football day, for the Panthers. Everybody is into and happy to be a part of Panther madness, and that's great. Now's the moment where you can have a great time. Made the playoffs! Not just making the playoffs and then getting knocked out, but *movin' on*. And I know we're going to win! I'm not making a prediction, I just feel it. I want the Panthers to beat St. Louis, and I want the Green Bay Packers to win. If that happens, the NFC Championship comes here. Panthers and Packers!

"I was talking with Kevin Donnalley yesterday at Hope's service. He is totally focused on this game. 'We have to do the job at hand,' is what he said.

"Kevin was also saying he's been doing more interviews with more people wanting to talk about Hope. He was interviewed yesterday by a radio station in Denver. ABC News is planning a story, and the contributions continue to roll in.

"But it's not strictly the money or the wishes. If you read Hope's webpage at CaringBridge, you find that in the last few days, something like 20,000 or 25,000 more visits have been made by people reading Hope's story and leaving messages of prayer and heartache and inspiration.

"It just seems to me, this girl, Hope, had too much love in her heart, and purpose in her life, to be held back by something as run of the mill as dying. I mean, we're all going to die. That's not a particularly special occurrence. But how many of us are going to change lives? How many of us are going to mesmerize countless thousands even afterward?

"And I know some people say Hope still lives, but to me, it's more like *Hope keeps rockin' on.*

"More than $600,000 has now been raised to help fulfill her wish."

IT HAD BEEN A HELL OF A WEEK. The unexpected Cinderella of the NFL season had launched into Playoffs 2003 with a convincing win over the Dallas Cowboys, ABC granting the never-officially-made wish of Hope Stout to be famous during the broadcast. From the high of the Panthers' win and Hope's stardom, to the depths of despair in just 24 hours, as the girl who had brought hope to the hopeless, died. The Stouts and the Carolinas said their final goodbye to the little redhead who had captured their hearts twelve years, or 21 days, earlier.

Yet those days of mourning were also filled with story after story of kids, neighborhoods, schools, and businesses breaking piggy banks, holding walk-a-thons and silent auctions, and taking collections to raise money for Hope's wish. One of the emails I received that week was from a family who lost their own son to cerebral palsy just a few years earlier. They had started a memorial fund in his honor that bought wheelchair-accessible vans and other conveniences for families with special needs kids. This couple told me they had heard my conversation with Hope and had each, separately, come to the same conclusion. After four years, it was time to close their son's charity and donate the remaining balance to grant Hope's wish. They had just mailed a check for $21,425.

The City of Charlotte had announced a big event uptown for Saturday at the Gateway Village center to watch the Panthers-Rams game on giant TV screens. They were calling it "Wish for a Panthers' Victory." It would be a fundraiser in Hope's honor. Thousands were expected, which would hopefully put a dent in the $400,000 still needed.

Cancer may have won its battle over Hope's body, but it had never stood a chance against her spirit. Hope was gone, but her spirit and her wish were alive. And because she had been such a fan, that spirit was now wrapped snuggly around Kevin Donnalley and the Panthers, who were alive in the playoffs. It had all become one beautiful blur. On Friday, January 9, the Celebration of Hope was only a week away, and the Cardiac Cats were boarding a plane for St. Louis.

# CHAPTER 22

# THE GREATEST SHOW ON TURF

IT WOULD BE AN EXAGGERATION to say that Charlotte looked like a ghost town at 4:30 the afternoon of Saturday, January 10, but not by much. It had felt like an all-day pep rally, with Panther hats and jerseys, and car flags and decals everywhere, but by midafternoon, people were packing homes and sports bars for the away-game edition of Panthers tailgating. One place fans weren't gathering was Gateway Village in uptown Charlotte.

There was a long-standing NFL rule against large group viewings of games. In an occurrence not at all uncommon in Charlotte, the uptown crowd had gotten ahead of itself. The city had never gotten approval to show the game at Gateway Village. Late Friday, the league put the kibosh on the city's big plans.

It was immensely disappointing and a missed opportunity to collect donations. More than $400,000 was still needed, and it was less than a week until the Celebration of Hope. Yet, even though it was city officials and uptown boosters who were wrong for hyping an event they'd never been authorized to hold, the NFL came off as the villain. A little girl dying of cancer had made a selfless, unheard of wish, and for three weeks, it seemed every ear that heard her voice, and heart that felt her call, had embraced her. Only cancer had been so cold as to spurn the spirit of Hope. Until now.

The League. That *Billionaires Club*, was putting TV rights and ad money ahead of the wishes of scores of sick children. It had the feeling of some corporate giant squashing a kid's lemonade stand. What the league's decision had really done was bind together all the more tightly Hope and her wish and the Panthers heading toward kickoff in St. Louis.

THEY CALLED THEMSELVES "The Greatest Show on Turf." The lack of modesty may have grated on opposing fans, but lately, it had been tough to dispute. The St. Louis Rams had made the playoffs three of the last four seasons, gone to the Super Bowl twice, and won it once. They had slipped to 7-9 in 2002, but rebounded mightily in 2003. They finished 12-4, were the number one scoring team in the league, and were on a wickedly hot roll in their home stadium.

"The Ed" it was called, with a braggadocio befitting a team whose first name was "Greatest." The Edward Jones Dome. Numbingly loud and notoriously nasty to visiting teams, the Rams had won fourteen straight there; a streak stretching almost two years. They were favored by a touchdown to win number fifteen – the heaviest playoff favorite of the weekend – as they lined up across from the Panthers on The Ed's spongy, deep-green artificial turf.

It would become the fifth longest game in NFL history. Riding on it were the Super Bowl hopes of two teams, the hopes of millions of fans, and the spirit of a little girl's wish.

THE PANTHERS WON the coin toss and chose to receive. The thinking was obvious. Don't give the explosive St. Louis offense first crack at the ball while the crazed fans in The Ed were riding the high of the start of the game. Less than three minutes later, the Panthers were punting.

They had opened in very un-Panther-like fashion, calling passes and gadget plays, which the St. Louis defense swiftly shut down. Instead of quieting the mob in The Ed, John Fox and the Panthers started the game by going for broke, breaking, and giving the crowd something to really cheer about. The Rams' offense picked the baton right up.

Quarterback Marc Bulger briskly completed pass after pass, all the way to the Panther 7-yard line where St. Louis coach Mike Martz turned curiously cautious. Three consecutive run plays, each stopped cold. They didn't throw even one pass, though passing had gotten them there. They hit the scoreboard first with a field goal, but it had looked like a touchdown was in the bag. Fans were not happy. The Ed was quieted in the game's first few minutes all right, but not by the Panthers.

The Rams drove inside the Carolina 20-yard line twice more in the first half, but each time, the Panther defense forced them to settle for a field goal. The Panthers scored the game's first touchdown on a bizarre play when a Jake Delhomme flip to a running back near the goal line was fumbled and recovered by Carolina receiver Muhsin Muhammad in the end zone.

With a slim 9-7 lead and seven minutes left in the first half, Mike Martz reached into the trick bag. He had turned oddly meek on play-calling each time the Rams got inside the Panther 20, but when the Rams kicked off after their third field goal, Martz called a surprise "pooch play." The idea is to boot the ball short – pooch it – so that it has to be caught by someone other than the receiving team's designated return man. The hope of the pooch is for a fumble that the kicking team will be poised to recover themselves, but as a trick play, it's an old dog. Receiving teams typically line up a player who's used to handling the ball between the deep man and the blockers for just such a ploy. For the Panthers, that was running back Brad Hoover, and he wasn't surprised in the slightest. He handled the ball cleanly and ran 19 yards to the 41. When the popular running back makes a big play in Panther Stadium, the crowd fills it with a resounding *HOOOO*-Ver, but the *OOOO*-ing that rose in The Ed was just plain *BOOOO*-ing, as fans let Mike Martz know what they thought of the pooch.

Jake Delhomme moved the Panthers inside the St. Louis 20 on four plays. They were poised to score. Then, on second down, DeShaun Foster took a Delhomme handoff and pounded to the 15. Penalty flag. The sound of the referee's wireless microphone clicking on crackled through the arena.

"Holding. Offense. Number 65. Ten-yard penalty. Still second down."

Kevin Donnalley. Penalties happen and they're never welcome, but that call on Donnalley set back a Panther touchdown drive and twisted a little knot in the stomachs of fans. On the replay, it looked like he had laid out a clean block, but the call had been made. It wiped out Foster's run and moved the Panthers back to almost the 30-yard line.

Second and 12. Jake passed to Jermaine Wiggins, who was prevented by a defender from even getting to the ball.

"Holding. Defense. Number 52. Five-yard penalty. Automatic first down."

A gift. Half of Donnalley's penalty yards were gained back, and the Panthers got a clean start, first and ten from the 24. Hand-off again to Foster, who this time, plowed all the way to the 12. Another flag.

"Personal foul. Major face mask on the offense. Number 65. Fifteen-yard penalty. Remains first down."

Donnalley again. Damn. When offensive linemen get TV close-ups it's almost never good. Kevin didn't want the first, and he seriously didn't want the second.

Three minutes left in the first half. Carolina had backpedalled from the St. Louis 12-yard line all the way back to the 39. Delhomme dropped back to pass, threw toward the far side of the field and ANOTHER FLAG.

"Holding."

No.

"Offense. Number 65."

Donnalley *again?*

"Ten-yard penalty. Still first down."

Oh my God.

Four plays, three penalties on Kevin Donnalley. Thirty-five penalty yards racked up by one offensive lineman on a scoring drive in a second-round playoff game. Unheard of. The look on Donnalley's face was not of a human expression. It was a contorted fighting back of wretched disgust at the referees and at himself. The calls were questionable. John Fox called a timeout just to rail at the officials. But as a thirteen-year veteran, Donnalley knew with all the hand-to-body combat, a flag can be thrown on an offensive lineman on practically any given play, so you *just can't* hold your guy. Even if you're not holding your guy, you *can't do* anything that makes a ref even *think* you *might* be holding him. And if you do hold your guy, you *just can't* get caught. Three times on camera, and the glare Donnalley flashed straight into its lens as he walked off the field could have made it cry. Carolina fans were close to crying themselves, and not just because they were seeing a great chance for a touchdown tossed away with the penalty flags.

They knew Hope Stout's name was written on Kevin Donnalley's gloves. They knew her spirit was pounding in his heart. Their hopes for her wish – and for a win by the underdog Panthers – were riding, in no small part, on his big shoulders. He was Hope's guy, and fans knew it. Even if they were frustrated over his penalties, they felt it in the gut for him.

The Panthers scratched back close enough for a field goal and a 10-9 lead. If someone had offered before the game that Carolina could go into halftime leading the Rams, even by just a point, any Panther or Panther fan would have taken it for certain. But to have left four additional points on the field, having given referees anything at all to throw a flag at, felt ominously uncertain.

TO START THE THIRD QUARTER, the Rams marched downfield but again were stopped short of the end zone. Kicker Jeff Wilkins came through with a field goal that snatched back the lead, 12-10, and fired The Ed back up. It cooled down fast. On the Panthers' next two possessions, John Kasay knocked through field goals, including a 52-yarder, to put Carolina on top 16-12. "The Greatest Show on Turf" entered the fourth quarter on the short end of the score, but came out slinging.

Bang-bang passes from Marc Bulger for first downs. In an instant, the Rams looked every bit the league's number one offense. Bulger passed again, but this time wildly overthrew star running back, Marshall Faulk. Panther safety Mike Minter settled underneath the ball as though he was the intended receiver, and The Ed went silent again.

Starting from their own 27 after the interception, the Panthers' offensive line blew open gaping holes for runs.

With plenty of Fat Cat protection, Jake Delhomme delivered a strike to a streaking Steve Smith, who ran a route called "X-clown." If they call it that because Smith takes off in one direction, crosses over in another to split the two defenders covering him, and then bolts in between them for the catch – making them look like clowns – it is aptly named. Smith was finally brought down after a 36-yard gain.

Minutes later, from the 7, Jeff Mitchell, Kevin Donnalley, and Jordan Gross formed a wedge that pushed the left side of the St. Louis defense almost all the way back across their own goal line. It was a cake-walk touchdown for Brad Hoover. With less than nine minutes left in the game, the Panthers had a 23-12 lead and had The Ed in abject shock.

And what comes after abject shock? The Rams' deep men botched the Panthers' kickoff. They let the ball bounce into their own end zone and were lucky the Panthers didn't fall on it for another touchdown. The very next play, Bulger threw desperately to receiver Torry Holt and was picked off again. As Rams' fans screamed for the head of the now twice-intercepted Marc Bulger, Carolina drove to the St. Louis 24. It would be a comfortable 42-yard field goal for John Kasay.

No one had imagined this. The underdog Panthers were about to kick a field goal to grab a fourteen-point, two-touchdown lead, with less than seven minutes to go. It would ice the game. To knock a few more seconds off the clock and a few more yards off the field goal distance, Fox decided to try one more play.

But why a pass? Rather than call a safe run play, the coaches had Jake drop back to throw. As he did, a defender slipped between Donnalley and Gross and dropped Delhomme for a big loss. The field goal to ice the Rams would now have to travel a booming 53 yards. It did. And if goal posts were 19-feet apart instead of 18-feet-6-inches, Kasay's kick would have sailed through for three points instead of bouncing off the left upright.

The Rams had caught a break, but they would still need to catch Carolina. The Panthers were up by eleven. To tie, St. Louis would need a touchdown, capped off by a two-point conversion, and a field goal. And they would have to get the ball back quickly in between. There were just over six minutes left. Getting the touchdown took four. The Rams got the two-point conversion easily on a short pass.

How many turns could one game take? The Panthers had the lead halfway through the fourth quarter, and could have locked it up, but blew it. Now, the Rams could send the game into overtime with a field goal or even go for another touchdown and the win, if they could get the ball back immediately with an onside kick. Those succeed only twenty percent of the time.

So much for percentages. The Rams got the ball back at the 42-yard line. A game-winning touchdown was only 58 yards away and more than two and a half minutes remained. They had one timeout; plus, the clock would automatically stop at the two-minute warning before the end of the game. Plenty of time.

The Rams drove easily to the Panther 15 without using their timeout and without ever having seemed in any rush. They had over thirty seconds left to go for a touchdown, two maybe three times, before settling for a field goal and the tie. Expectant cheers rising in The Ed urged the Rams to go for it. The cheers U-turned into howling boos as Martz let the clock run down to three seconds and called for the field goal unit. He'd been playing for the tie all along.

A FIFTH PLAYOFF QUARTER. Sudden Death Overtime. A new fifteen minutes on the clock, but the clock didn't really matter anymore. It was 23-23, but *points* didn't really matter anymore. The next team to score would win, and they would play until one did.

The coin toss to start the overtime again fell the Panthers' way, and again, they got the ball first. Instant hope. When they took only four plays to drive to field goal range inside the St. Louis 20, hope turned to anxious expectation. And when John Kasay's kick traveled straight through the uprights, anxious expectation exploded into glorious celebration. Panthers leaped into the air, arms raised straight overhead, making the "good" signal. Fans did the same. Players and coaches rushed onto the field jumping with joy. They hadn't seen the penalty flag.

No one had. It was dropped far behind the action by the official whose job it is to watch the play clock. From the moment the referee officially sets the ball in play, the offensive team has 25 seconds to commence. The official had been eyeing the ticking clock, but the Panthers hadn't. It had run down, and the flag had been thrown just before the ball was snapped. The replay showed it clearly. Life drained from the celebrating Panthers' faces. Fans' faces mirrored the players.

How much cardiac could a team and its faithful take in one game? In one season? With the 5-yard delay of game penalty, the kick would now be 45 yards.

It curved just outside the right goal post. This time it was the Rams who leaped into the air and ran onto the field, and this time there was no penalty flag to cause a do-over. Another heart attack for Panther fans, and this felt like "the big one."

St. Louis got the ball and with one pass, blasted into Jeff Wilkins's field goal range. It would be a 53, maybe 54-yard kick. Now it was Rams' fans that were filled with anxious expectation. But Martz left them flabbergasted again by not doing much of anything to try to cut that distance. If they had picked up just a couple of yards, Wilkins's kick would have cleared the crossbar instead of falling just short. Now, it was life draining from the faces of St. Louis players and fans, which the cameras caught.

Carolina got the ball back on their 43-yard line. To reach John Kasay field goal distance, they would need about 20 yards. They got 22 when Jake Delhomme fired to Muhsin Muhammad on their first play. The Panthers could go for the win right now, but John Fox had seen Mike Martz send Jeff Wilkins up to try a game-winner from a couple yards too far just two plays earlier. He decided he wanted to get a little closer before sending Kasay up to kick.

Damn déjà vu! Just as when Fox wanted Kasay a couple yards closer for the "ice-it" field goal try in the fourth quarter – *why a pass?* The Rams front line tore past the Fat Cats and sacked Delhomme far out of field goal range.

Now the Panthers *had* to go for more yards – big yards. But on their next play, a penalty. Then the Rams' defense plowed through Donnalley and company and batted down a Delhomme pass. By third down, the Panthers had been pushed back to almost the 50-yard line; way out of field goal range. They had to pass, and St. Louis knew it. The rush the Rams put on the Panthers was merciless. The Fat Cats were flattened; Jake along with them. He slammed the ball in disgust and stormed off the field as the punting unit came on.

Maddening game! The Panthers nearly had it locked in the fourth quarter, and the Rams also had a great chance to win. In overtime, each team missed winning field goals, and the Panthers had just squandered a chance at another. The game had gone from grinding to thrilling to baffling, with tension rising beyond bearable.

Off the Panther punt, St. Louis got the ball on their own 13 and would need to go 50 yards before they could even think about calling on Jeff Wilkins again. They ripped off 49 yards in five plays, down to the Carolina 38. The field goal try would be 55 yards. Truly, too long. Martz knew he needed five more to send in Wilkins comfortably. It was first down, and he had three plays to get the 5.

The 65,000 people still in The Ed, and the millions watching on TV, may have been surprised when Marc Bulger took the next snap and dropped back deep, looking to pass downfield, but Ricky Manning was not. The rookie Panther cornerback reached in front of Rams receiver Torry Holt for a one-handed interception.

Stunned. Jaw-dropping stunned, the Rams and their fans. *Why* would Mike Martz have Bulger throw long on first down having played so cautiously all day? They didn't need a touchdown to win. They didn't even need big yardage for a field goal, so why? Element of surprise? Redemption? All anyone knew for sure was, it was a mistake. Fans broke into enraged booing and hollering. Martz must have been glad for the wall and the stadium security that rings the field.

Jake and the Panther offense returned to the field sensing victory, but St. Louis's shredding of the Fat Cats continued. On first down, the O-line was bowled over and running back DeShaun Foster was thrown for a loss. On second down the Rams blitzed. Jake was sacked again. As Delhomme pulled himself up off the ground and held his hands over his head, pleading for protection, the gun sounded a merciful end to the fifth quarter.

What next? What else? Who had anything left in this bizarre mini-series that was about to become the first double-overtime playoff game in the National Football League in sixteen years? Each team was desperate to win, yet neither was getting it won. Fatigued fans could barely stand any longer, but sitting was not an option. How could the players possibly play? The Rams and Panthers were like two punch-drunk boxers gone, somehow, into a sixteenth and then seventeenth round of a fight tied on points, each with arms dangling, unable to raise a glove, but needing a knockout punch to win.

Or an X-clown.

SIXTH QUARTER. Play continues. Another new 15:00. Whatever. They'll put up as many 15:00s as it takes.

Panther ball; their own 31-yard line. Third down. They needed a long 14 yards for a first down to keep the drive alive. St. Louis put seven men up front to charge after Jake. He took the snap. The Rams cranked up the blitz. Delhomme scampered straight back to pass, and the Cats became Fat once again.

Todd Steussie, Jeno James, and Jeff Mitchell held off defenders to Jake's left. Jordan Gross pushed his man out to the right. Kevin Donnalley rose like a mountain in front of his quarterback and forced the St. Louis middle linebacker away. From the left side, Steve Smith lit off downfield. He took off in one direction, then crossed over in another to split the two defenders covering him, while he then *bolted in between…*

X-clown again!

Jake pumped and let loose a laser from his own 25. Smith made the grab in full stride at the 50 to burn desperately-diving defensive back Jason Sehorn and fly past linebacker Tommy Polly. He cut straight downfield and outran the rest of the Rams. Turning for a look back as he sprinted past the 25 to the 20 – seeing no penalty flags, knowing it was happening – Smith's arms, like wings, gloriously outstretched, as he passed the 10 to the 5. As he crossed the goal line, he looked gratefully to the heavens, as if they could be seen through the domed roof of the conclusively silenced Ed.

Victory! And with it, not merely happiness or even joy, but elation. Relieved, exhausted elation on the face and in the arms of Steve Smith. Elation gushed out of Jake Delhomme as he galloped up the field toward Smith in the end zone. Elated Panther players and coaches streamed onto the field and jumped into each other's arms. Elation, in homes and bars in the Carolinas, just as the stunned silence of the Rams and their fans in the stands, coursed throughout St. Louis and the Midwest.

In the Panther locker room, as jerseys were pulled off players and Polo shirts off coaches, there they were. The T-shirts: 58 and 51. Sam Mills and Mark Fields. Everywhere. The Panthers had kept pounding. Through six quarters of football, they kept pounding, kept pounding, kept pounding. They had pounded their way to the NFC Championship the next Sunday.

Two days before that, on Friday, January 16, 2004, Kevin Donnalley would have an appointment at the Westin Hotel in Charlotte. His date wouldn't make it to her celebration, but he would be there in her honor. And he wouldn't be going stag.

# CHAPTER 23

# PANTHERMONIUM

THE TEAM BUSES ROLLED into Panther Stadium parking from Charlotte airport in the middle-of-the-night darkness before Sunday was even a few hours old. They were met by thousands of fans braving the 25-degree cold to wave and cheer and welcome the team home – and to snap pictures as proof they had been there. It was the beginning of an off-the-hook week.

The NFC Championship Game was coming up the next Sunday. The Panthers would be in it, but they wouldn't be playing in front of seventy-some thousand fans in Charlotte. The Philadelphia Eagles hadn't gotten John Fox's memo. They didn't know they were supposed to lose to the Green Bay Packers so the Panthers could play the Pack in Charlotte and avenge their 1996 conference championship loss at frigid Lambeau Field.

The Eagles beat Green Bay by a field goal in overtime. The Panthers would be playing for a spot in the Super Bowl in Philadelphia against the Eagles, not in Charlotte against the Packers.

THERE MUST HAVE BEEN people in the Carolinas who hadn't watched the Panthers-Rams nail-biter of a marathon Saturday night, as there must have been people who hadn't watched Neil Armstrong walk on the moon, but who? And any who hadn't would surely come to believe they had, with all the telling and retelling of the kicks and misses, the touchdowns and interceptions, the penalties, the baffling coaching, and that final exalting X-clown. Replays were shown continually on TV and played like a top-forty hit on the radio. The picture of Steve Smith gloriously crossing the goal line for the win, stretched in newsprint color across both the front page and the sports page of the *Charlotte Observer*. The game and the win quickly became part of the Carolinas' consciousness, whether one had seen it live or not.

The idyllic exuberance wasn't to be basked in for long. A scathing, taunting rip on Charlotte ran in Monday morning's *Philadelphia Daily News*. There's no such thing as a *local* newspaper in the internet age, so I had the column, read it on the air, and had it linked to my website by a few minutes after nine o'clock.

## In our mind, there's nothing in Carolina

By Will Bunch

Charlotte – hometown of the Carolina Panthers – is a sprawling, ugly Sunbelt City that looks a lot like Atlanta. But Atlanta was once "the city too busy to hate." Charlotte is the city too easy to hate.

This endless and soul-less NASCAR hypnotized expanse of strip malls and

Shoney's finally got its pro franchise
when the NFL finally ran out of real cities
somewhere between Jacksonville, Fla., and
Nashville, Tenn. However, there is one
area where the Carolinas can lay claim to
major league status: The self-righteous
hypocrisy of its rogue's gallery of
unreformed segregationists and Bible
thumping con artists.

That was only the beginning. The column tore fiercely
into the city of Charlotte and the people of the Carolinas.
It bashed bankers and basketball team owners; took aim at
typical targets Jim and Tammy Faye Bakker, Billy Graham,
Jesse Helms, and Strom Thurmond; recounted a few felons
among former Panthers; and turned the city's own civic
silliness on itself by quoting an online list of things to do
around town called "Connection Charlotte" that actually
suggests "visiting the library" and "going shoe shopping."
It was a big-city slashing of a big small town that wanted
desperately to sit at the table with the adults. It must have
had them belly-laughing in South Philly and Roxborough
and Manayunk. The go-for-the-throat column wouldn't
have phased Chicagoans used to Mike Royko or New
Yorkers, Jimmy Breslin, but Bunch's was an amateur work
by comparison. His final salutation – simply the letters "F.
U."– was a conclusion far too unimaginatively crude to ever
have been dignified in print by the two Pulitzer Prize winners.

The column was a hack job but it did the job, and I knew
how it was going to make people feel. I knew every instinct
and reflex of anyone in Charlotte who read it would be, *OH
YEAH!?* and to try to hit back. But I'm from Chicago. I
grew up on Royko. I knew nothing would make Will Bunch
and the Philadelphians he Pied Pipered happier than to get

Charlotte's goat and see Charlotteans throwing desperate verbal punches in flailing retaliation.

I tried to head off revenge using martial arts, by not striking back at Bunch directly but through finesse, using the obesity of his column against him. My producer, Mark, convinced him to come on the show late Tuesday. Earlier that morning I had explained to listeners what we were going to do. There'd be no punching back, no name calling, no *OH YEAH!?* I said I wanted people to call in and play right into Will Bunch's characterization of Charlotte as a boring, hick town. Make us out, not even as Mayberry, but Hooterville. We held rehearsals early in the show, and people called back in later when Bunch was on.

They invited Bunch – who said he had been through Charlotte airport but had never stepped outside it – to come back to town because *we now have indoor plumbing*. A guy invited him to go catfish fishing; a lady, to come see her new drapes. Callers thanked Bunch for Philadelphia Cream Cheese and invited him to come set a spell on their front porch in a rocker and watch the trains go by. Callers were perfect, Bunch was flustered, and it was priceless.

More than 2,000 Carolinians still emailed him though. Bunch's Wednesday column was an expanded piece *filled* with desperate verbal punches thrown by Charlotteans in flailing retaliation. They called him an idiot, called Philadelphia rude, and called Philadelphians "Yankees." It hurt to read it on the air knowing how gleefully the sequel would have been received in South Philly and Roxborough and Manayunk. The Piper predictably gave no hint to his mice of his skittish performance or the nuanced thumping he took from my listeners. Will Bunch's piece on Wednesday was tough to swallow, but the announcement on the Carolina Panthers' website that morning went down smoothly.

Each week during the season, the Panthers name a "Fan of the Week." On Wednesday, January 14, the team website displayed a picture of a big offensive lineman with his arms around two girls in Panther jerseys. One of the girls – the one in the center of the picture and to the player's left – stood propped by crutches not entirely hidden by the long tails of the white scarf looped so casually perfect around her neck, her hair cascading from a black bandana, a mom and dad next to her with arms around each other. Kevin Donnalley with Hope and Emily, and Stuart and Shelby, on the sidelines of Panther Stadium before the Tennessee game – five shining smiles, ten eyes squinting into the sun.

"Our fan of the week, and our fan of any week, is Hope Stout… the courageous young girl who recently lost her life to cancer," the story opened. She looked so alive, so bright and sparkling in the picture, riding her VP-16 high that spectacular weekend. The piece told of Hope's cancer battle, her wish, and her special Panther. It was easy to wonder what Will Bunch and his minions might think.

As the week wended along, the pitch in Charlotte stoked to a fever for the NFC Championship Game and for the Celebration of Hope. On the show I kept reading emails, taking calls, giving updates; talking about all things Hope and wishes and Panthers and playoffs. Donations kept rolling in to Make-A-Wish, and random acts of lighted-candle fundraising kept happening. The *Charlotte Observer* pictured two young south Charlotte girls pulling a wagon through their neighborhood. They were bugged that the uptown viewing party for the St. Louis game had been cancelled and wanted to help, so they were selling cups of hot chocolate door to door. They raised $1,117.54. The sports pages and sports shows covered each Panther practice and all the preparations for Philadelphia. Every detail was digested.

Friday morning, the headline of the *Observer* shouted **"PANTHERMONIUM!"** And by late that morning there was Panthermonium overflowing from uptown.

Charlotte does love its pep rallies, and the center city crowd has a hair trigger for calling them. The one called for the Friday before the NFL Conference Championship Game though – a game that can send your team to the Super Bowl – *that* pep rally is justified. The thousands filling the square at Trade and Tryon Streets in the heart of uptown knew it and let it show. They came decked out in full game-day regalia, customized for the chilly 40-degree morning. They wore Panther jerseys and team sweatshirts with base layers underneath; hats and giant blue foam Panther claws. Streaming pom poms and big "D-FENSE" signs were waved; posters and placards were pumped up and down. Sir Purr and the TopCat dancers got the crowd gyrating to Ted Nugent's guitar on "Cat Scratch Fever," the semi-official Panther theme, as it pulsed out of giant speakers and echoed off shiny skyscrapers.

Panther players couldn't attend as the team was going through its last practice before the trip to Philadelphia. It was left to the Panthers' spirit squad and Charlotte Mayor, Pat McCrory, to lead the rally. With the crowd so willing to be whipped up, they had no difficulty. When the mayor made the surprise announcement that two players had briefly been cut loose from practice to represent the team, fans went wild. "*HOOOO-VER*" filled the air as running back Brad Hoover bounded on stage in his practice jersey. Then, along with the cheers, a warming wave of emotion surged through the crowd as big number 65 appeared. Everyone knew why Kevin Donnalley was there. By Friday, January 16, 2004, there was no clear line between the Carolina Panthers and Hope Stout's wish. Donnalley ratified the union before the thousands that filled uptown for the city's official send-off for the team as he brought Holly, Austin, Shelby, and Stuart Stout on stage.

If applause could heal.

I'd had Stuart and Kevin on the show together that morning. Stuart was calm and strong, talking about everything Hope and his family had been through and how hard it had been the last ten days not seeing her – but how surely he had felt her presence. He was upbeat and optimistic, talking about all that was happening with her wish. It was "like trying to take a drink from a fire hydrant," Stuart said.

Donnalley was open and humble, reminiscing about meeting Hope before the Tennessee game and what she had come to mean to him and the Panthers; how thinking of her helped get him through the St. Louis game and that stretch when penalties made *him* a TV star. He was confident, but careful, talking about the Philadelphia game coming up in two days. He said the Panthers seemed to be the forgotten team among the four remaining and were being written off. It was feeling, Kevin said, "Like a perfect script to go to Philly and make Charlotte proud."

Earlier that morning, Google let me know there was a story about Hope and her wish and the Panthers in a paper in Munich, Germany. It was four weeks to the day since she had told me, "It's gonna happen."

# CHAPTER 24

# THE CELEBRATION OF HOPE

OUT IN FRONT of the dazzling new Westin Hotel in uptown Charlotte, Friday night, powerful floodlights darted across an ebony January sky. Shiny cars – a healthy mix of limousines among them – rolled up the oval, inlaid-brick boulevard around the fountain and the flagpoles. They dropped off fares at the door or were left in the custody of valets. Women and girls legged out one high heel at a time into a frosty Carolina night. They shivered to the door, or pulled on jackets or wraps, over gowns that bared arms and backs and shoulders; the ladies dressed for the ambience of the glittering ballroom rather than those few frigid seconds of winter chill. Splendid, gallant men attired in the customary manner, identical but for occasional impulses of individuality in ties, cummerbunds, and vests, offered hands of help to their *dames*. It was a Rat Pack theme. That's what Hope had wanted.

Inside the hotel foyer: the red carpet. Cameras flashed as fast as smiles. Guests swarmed the check-in and got their IDs, then streamed onto the wide escalator and rode to the royal entrance of the Promenade reception hall surrounding the ballroom. Chilled shrimp, caviar, and salmon tartare, and cheeses and crackers and finger-food delicacies, along with cocktails, champagne, and wine – refreshed and warmed to a glow. Refrains of 1950s Doo Wop from Carmine and the Blue Moons wafted through the Promenade; inside, "Under My Skin" and other strains of Frank Nazarro's classy, understated Sinatra Experience set the tone.

The 16,277-square-foot Grand Ballroom was decked with scores of big round tables covered in crisp white linens and fluted vases that held white orchids and pink tulips. Dozens of balloons in pastel pink and blue dotted the perimeter; silver stars dangled from their ribbon tethers. A glamorous, glassy stage backed by a black scrim curtain, jeweled in a universe of twinkling lights, stretched across the front of the room. A giant yellow-gold shooting star streaked across with the words "Celebration of Hope" scripted in cursive on its arching tail. Large acrylic plant stands bearing ample ferns bookended the platform. A grey marble-esque podium, fronted by a smaller "Celebration of Hope" shooting star, stood in the center. Onto super-sized screens, to the left and right of the platform, splashed the in-house video, which would turn the on-stage proceedings larger than life for those seated in the further reaches of the great hall.

They had planned the $250-a-ticket party hoping, praying, they could get 750 sold. Days before, the number pushed 900. By that night, it was an overflow. Working on a million-dollar wish, no one with a check had been turned away. With the Grand Ballroom packed, the hotel scrambled to convert the Promenade to cocktail-table seating and kept the doors to the ballroom open.

The din had risen to a roar by go time. Individual conversations were indistinguishable except for widely repeated variations on the theme, *Can you believe this? If only Hope could see this.* The room was electric, electrified. Everyone buzzed and connected comprehensively by emotions shooting from all corners of the heart: amazement, over a little girl's wish; wonder, over all that had happened in just four weeks; bliss, in the resplendent brilliance of the event itself; anticipation, and also anxiousness, for the evening to unfold. And at some point, it was assumed, a grand total would be announced. Yet it all hung on the edge of an inescapable ache.

Hope was gone. She had died only twelve days earlier. The fabulous night was proof that cancer never stood a chance against Hope's spirit but also as confirmation it had won its battle over her body. Along with the euphoria of the night was a feeling like that moment at the church – at Hope's service – just before the Stouts entered. So much emotion pent up tightly inside hearts stretched as thin as the rubber of the balloons along the walls, hanging thick and heavy all through the room. When there's a celebration, everyone celebrates; when there's a hurt, everyone hurts. I could feel it on stage.

"GOOD EVENING EVERYBODY, and welcome to this incredible Celebration of Hope."

At some point along the way, they had asked me to host the event.

"Like you, I am here having been mesmerized by Hope Stout. I have not, in the last four weeks, figured out how else to describe it." No one had.

"This particular part of the Hope story, tonight's Celebration of Hope, actually began about two months ago. I'd like to read from the *Charlotte Observer* of one month ago, December 19… Elizabeth Leland's story:

"'When Make-A-Wish Foundation asked 12-year-old Hope Stout what she wanted, instead of answering, Hope asked a question. "How many children are waiting on wishes?"

'Another 155 they told her.' "My wish," Hope said, "is to help raise the money to grant all of their wishes.'"

"Well, take a look around. You are seeing tonight the party Hope envisioned. She wanted an elegant Hollywood-style bash with a lot of fun and the flavor of the Rat Pack era, complete with Ol' Blue Eyes himself. And we came pretty close.

"I know that… everyone… wished and prayed Hope would be here with us tonight.

"I know Kevin Donnalley *likes the guys* he's here with tonight but would rather have had his intended escort. He does have his wife, Erica, with him and has been escorted by Panthers Todd Steussie and Jeff Mitchell."

Cautious applause. The room was tense, uncertain.

"Let's give them a hand."

More appropriate clapping.

Quiet returned. I paused.

And then with a quick cock of the head and the crack of a smile…

"*They have an APPOINTMENT in a couple of days!*"

Now cheers. Unrestrained applause. Joyful noise filled the air.

People near the three Carolina Panthers rose, applauding over them. When the Panthers themselves rose, thunder rolled. Glasses were raised; the house lights came up. Everyone was standing.

The wave subsided. In its wake, release. The gushing over the Panthers lanced the tension in the room. Of course it did. Hope would have been leading the cheers.

I turned back toward the Fat Cats.

"Kevin Donnalley's support for Hope Stout and her family and this Celebration tonight has been outstanding, and it's absolutely great that he and some of the other Panthers are able to be here. Everyone's wish would be that Hope would be with us. But as her mother, Shelby, said recently, 'Hope, tonight, has the best seat in the house.'"

A couple thousand or so hands agreed.

I introduced the Reverend Ken Lyon. The slight, lightly salt-and-peppered pastor with the brush of a beard and glasses strode gently to the podium. In the same way the Stouts' faith was not something they wore only on Sundays, Ken Lyon was not a man of simplistic religious bromides. He would help them find true encouragement in the life and words of Jesus, but he had also told them – that day in the hospital when he heard with them those first shattering syllables from Dr. Kneisl, "I'm afraid the news is not good" – that sometimes, life just stinks.

"God, we gather here tonight carrying images of Hope. We carry images of Hope as that beautiful, redheaded, courageous little girl whose compassion for others and generous spirit has touched our lives so deeply. We carry the images of Hope inspiring our own potential to carry out her wish, that scores upon scores of boys and girls might have their lives blessed, their burden of illness lightened, their families drawn toward joy in the face of awful circumstance. We carry the images of Hope as a sacred trust that in your keeping care, oh God, there is a promise that the worst this world can bring cannot ultimately separate us from your love or from your eternity that waits to wipe away every tearful goodbye with a joyful and glad reunion. So tonight, we celebrate. With glad and joyful and thankful hearts, we celebrate in Hope, for Hope, with Hope. Amen."

Ken Lyon could soften the soul of the soulless.

"We also have here with us tonight, the Mayor of the City of Charlotte, Pat McCrory." Charlotte's youngish mayor looked like Harry Potter at age forty.

"Kevin Donnalley asked me not to do any more trash-talking toward the Eagles because he has to play against them this Sunday," the mayor laughed, "so I promised I wasn't going to say *one more bad word about those thugs*, that we're gonna *kick their...* in Philadelphia.

"What a pep rally today!" McCrory continued. "But I'll tell you... half the spirit was the spirit of Hope. There's no doubt about it!"

He was right.

To the crowd in the Grand Ballroom and the overflow standing at cocktail tables out in the Promenade, McCrory read the decree he had made to the thousands in the square that morning. "It is my honor to proclaim January 16, 2004, as the Day of Hope." Raising high the booklet containing the document, McCrory looked to the Stouts and affirmed, "This is for Hope."

Such proclamations are, of course, standard daily fare for mayors, and commemorate the trivial as well as the meaningful. The hitch in McCrory's voice as he read the declaration, and the reverent reply of the assembly, left no doubt that this pronouncement had been made most sincerely and received quite the same way.

The marvelous epidemic that was Hope's wish had permeated every strata of society, so there were other politicians in the crowd: city council and county commission types, local congressmen. Politicians always require recognition, which was done by the host on behalf of the Stouts, thankfully and graciously – for the most part. I had also been given a letter, received from United States Senator John Edwards, a controversial figure even then.

"He was interested but was unable to be here.

"And the Stouts are thankful... for that."

It started slowly, from pockets around the room, the knowing laughter. Pause. Louder laughter. "That either came out all wrong or all right, depending on which side of the fence you're on." Howls of laughter.

I let the room settle.

"LADIES AND GENTLEMEN, we have a story to tell you tonight. It is the story of a courageous little girl and the power of a wish."

The lights went down. The vast hall became intensely dark.

The universe appeared on the large video screens. Flickering lights from distant galaxies rushed into the expanse as the cadence of crickets chirping in the night filled the room. The gentle, knowing voice of a father floated in.

"Sure is pretty out here."

Followed by the sweet confirmation of a trusting child.

"Mm hm."

There materialized a white glow.

"Look, there's the first star." Its rays darting a dancing escape from its pulsing body.

"Mm hm."

"You know what to do? Close your eyes, and make a wish."

The star shot off, and suddenly, there appeared Hope's cousin, Liz Reeder, and best friend, Emily Rutherford.

"Hope is… just an incredible person," Liz said, with a toss of her head and a wide smile, her eyes beaming as she thought of her close cuz. "She's got a bubbly personality. She's an inspiration to everybody."

"When I think of Hope, I think of a happy person who helps a lot of people," said Emily, with a reflective look in her eyes and introspection in her young voice.

"I think she's going to do a lot with her life."

They were young and pretty and thirteen years old, or about to be. Each wore the silver star charm designed by Hope that Make-A-Wish had been selling. They were saying Hope "*is* an incredible person," Hope "*is* going to do a lot with her life." They were speaking *presently*. She was alive yet. These were the interviews done the day after Hope had talked with me. The conversations taped at the Stouts' home just before she turned "gravely ill."

There was Stuart's cousin, Wendy Reeder, who'd been like a third parent to Hope; her husband Tom, almost a brother to Stuart; and Bruce Mullen, a long-time friend all but legally Hope's uncle. There was Courtney Plaisted, one of Hope's nurses; and case workers, Kelli Breaux and Lynne Allen who were the very first to visit her from Make-A-Wish.

Holly Stout spoke with certainty and serenity of Hope's faith. Austin, in wistful wonder of sitting back and watching Hope perform her magic. Hope's mom and dad appeared throughout the video, proud and pleased, though their pain was always in the shot.

And 310 pounds of Carolina Panther was still big, but less bulky, without the number 65 jersey with shoulder pads underneath.

"She crosses my mind all the time, every day... during games, in the middle of games. When I'm tired or something's wearing on me or I'm down, I think of her. And she, like her name, just gives me hope." Kevin Donnalley's eyes assured he was telling the truth, though his sheepish smile hinted that he, too, was astonished at how a little girl he had only known briefly had consumed him so completely.

Finally, the screens and the room fell dark once again. The universe and rushing stars and crickets returned. Exhale. An affecting journey of the heart through effected people opening theirs. Close call, but we'd made it. Yet shouldn't we have known there was one still to appear?

Out of the cosmos and over the crickets came, once more, the voice of the child.

"Star light, star bright, first star I see tonight."

*Oh Jesus.*

"Wish I may, wish I might…"

*Piercing the darkness, she filled the screen.*

Lying in her hospital bed at home, she was propped up on a sea foam-green pillow, covered by a soft pink blanket, surrounded by stuffed animals, holding a fuzzy golden bear; blazing red wig, its locks flipped up at her shoulders, wrapped at her forehead by a rich blue bandana; silver star charm of her own design attached to a delicate chain, relaxed around the collar of her matching blue turtleneck. The freckles, the bright eyes…

"*My wish…*" the smile, as she lifted her head on cue, "is for all of the other kids to have their wish granted."

Hope. Alive. As alive and full of life as she would ever again be.

"We want these kids' wishes granted because some of them need it much more than I do, and I want my wish after I'm better," she said. Quickly adding with a sure shake of her head and secure smile, "and my wish is already coming true – to be famous and all," sparked ironic, relieved-to-laugh laughter around the room that lingered as she continued.

"Please help out and donate money or buy a Hope charm." She was off on her mission.

"Just know, whatever you do, know you made a difference in that kid's life… no matter if you donate five thousand dollars, or just… five! You've made a difference; just know that. Please help out because…"

As she spoke, that same something came over her, or alive in or through her, as when I had talked with her on the radio. She began speaking so assuredly and unequivocally, and as she did, the breathiness returned…

"These kids need this a lot more than a lot of us do because…"

*and forced a deliberate…*

"…we're so blessed…"

*inhaling breath…*

"…and they… they have to go through a lot."

*between every few words.*

"I know… because… I'm going through a lot too."

*Inhale.*

"Just… please help. It would mean so much to me, and…"

*Inhale.*

"…everyone else."

The camera froze. Not on a trademark beaming Hope smile, but on one smaller, subtler. It came as her close-up closed and brought a look to her eyes of one who knew, somehow, her work had finished. Our last look at the young star faded into a dazzling starburst and left the room with a soothing sense of surrender and a peaceful presence. Light shone again in the ballroom and revealed onstage, Stuart and Shelby Stout.

Thousands of clapping hands form quite a hug.

"GOD HAS GIVEN ME STRENGTH!" Shelby proclaimed profoundly, "because I have watched that about twenty times to try to get ready for tonight, and I've broken down every time but this. So I know God is with me right now – and, Hope."

Wearing a black, sequined gown that was its own glittering universe, and a black necklace with the silver Hope charm, Shelby said she needed to speak for Hope.

She thanked everyone from Carolinas Medical Center. "They got to know Hope, and *Hope didn't like the hospital.* So the way *we* know Hope, sometimes they didn't really know *that* Hope, 'cause she gave them a *hard time,*" Shelby admitted with a warm, sheepish smile. They were all there in the ballroom: Doctor Kneisl and Doctor McMahon and all of Hope's nurses. They stood humbly but obediently in response to a command from Shelby as the sound of appreciation washed over them.

"You all were really taking care of her, and she loved you very dearly. I want to thank you all for getting us through this hard time."

Shelby thanked all the kids in attendance. So many of Hope's friends were there: girls and boys, neighbors and classmates, and kids from church. They had put on fundraisers, bought or sold charms, prayed for her, and stood by her in so many different ways.

Finally, Shelby also thanked a guest who was one of the very first Hope had put on her VIP list for the night. She brought him out in front of the stage in his tuxedo coat and black top hat – Surfer, a deep-honey-brown and white Sheltie. Surfer was a trained therapy dog who had stayed often in Hope's room. He got her through when she missed her animals at home.

Maybe it was the lighting, or maybe it was the wash of his pridefully blushing cheeks, or tearfully reddened eyes, but Stuart Stout's strawberry-blonde hair looked even more strawberry than usual as he moved to the microphone after Shelby.

"Although Hope is not here physically, I know she is here in spirit. Many of you know she's here in spirit. Were she to walk in here and see this, I can see the smile from ear to ear. With two thumbs up, *Dad*, she would say, *this is way cool!*

"And I'm sure she would also say to Kevin and the rest of the Panthers, *Please take care of business on Sunday night.*"

No one tired of cheering for Hope and the Panthers.

"While this is a celebration of Hope, this is also a celebration of faith," Stuart continued with conviction. "Hope's story has no doubt moved many people to rekindle relationships with their family and with their God, our family included. But in doing so, we need to be mindful that faith without action is very hollow. Hope has left us all with a great challenge: to take the reborn faith we have all experienced and put it into action. Congratulations! She just made all of you missionaries!"

Consenting laughter.

"The pay isn't great, but I assure you, the rewards are out of this world!

"Jesus told us, from those to whom much is given, much is expected. Look around this room tonight and tell me we have not been given a lot. The challenge before us now is, what will *we* do? We've been given a good example."

Warm, wall-to-wall applause escorted Stuart and Shelby from the stage. No hands were idle. No one was left sitting, no eyes left dry.

"Thank you very much, Shelby and Stuart. I'm not good enough at this to have the words to convey what people here feel for Hope and for each of you and for your whole family, but... I hope you know. In looking around, in listening, in feeling it... I hope you know.

# CHAPTER 25

# A LITTLE FOOTBALL

"ALL RIGHT! *Ready for an auction?*" They were ready for the auction!

"We have spotters out and about to help see who's bidding and to encourage you to bid higher and bid more. You're going to have to wave your program to get the attention of the spotters. Let's everybody practice that. "Wave your program."

"WAVE... YOUR PROGRAM!

"WAVE... your credit card.

"WAVE... your check book."

Auctioneer Ernest Perry jumped right in and gave everybody the proper perspective. "Remember, you're not bidding tonight, you're donating. So let's not call it an auction."

We proceeded to not auction, but rather accept donations for, nine wide-ranging items, from a fabulous pearl necklace donated by Ernie Perry (in real life he owns a well-known Charlotte jewelry store), to a can't-get-it-just-anywhere NASCAR racing experience, including pit passes and a high-speed ride-along with one of the professional drivers. There was a jersey autographed by North Carolina resident and all-the-rage *American Idol* star Clay Aiken and four tickets to the Super Bowl in Houston given by Jerry Richardson out of the allotment the NFL gives every team owner. Each of the items sold for several thousand dollars. And then there was Kevin Donnalley's football.

"We don't have an estimated value on this next item up for bid, but I'll tell you what... it's going to be worth a lot more in 48 hours," I declared.

Expectant approval.

"And in two weeks and 48 hours."

Excited howls.

"Kevin Donnalley brought a little football with him, and it's got a *whole bunch of writing on it.*"

Eager cheers were released as one of the "Vanna Whites" of the auction appeared holding the football. It was brown and white leather with the snarling-panther logo and black magic marker scribbles all over. The ball was signed by the entire team – all the heroes of the Panthers' no-one-predicted-it cardiac run to the NFC Championship Game coming up in two days – including Jake Delhomme, Steve Smith, Julius Peppers, and of course, Kevin Donnalley, Jeff Mitchell, Todd Steussie, and the rest of the Fat Cats. It was the right item for the right night, and Ernie didn't waste a second.

"All right, what's your starting bid? A thousand dollars? Takes one thousand to bid. *Yes!* Who'll make it two and..."

A hand flashed.

"*Now* three. I have two and *now* three to bid. It takes *three* thousand to bid. Who'll go to *three?*"

Perry pointed affirmatively at a spotter.

"And *now* four. Will you bid *four* thousand? I have *three* and now it takes *four* thousand. Will you *bid* four? *YES!* And *now* five. Will you *bid* five? Takes *five* to bid. Who'll go *five? YES!* And *NOW* six!"

Ernie was ripping through his script.

"I have five and *now* six. Who'll go *six* thousand? *YES!* And *NOW* seven. Takes seven to be able to bid. Seven *thousand* dollars; a great donation tonight. *YES!* And *NOW* EIGHT!"

Seven thousand dollars in 25 seconds. The bidding was quickly dominated by two hands. One to Perry's left, and one to his right. The showdown allowed Ernie to really go to work.

"Takes *EIGHT* to bid, go *EIGHT* THOUSAND."

Pointing directly at the bidders.

"EIGHT, back to you at *EIGHT* THOUSAND. Kevin's going to bring it to you personally, whoever gets the winning donation, I promise you! I have seven, I'm asking eight… and *NOW* I *HAVE* EIGHT! And NOW *NINE* THOUSAND. Will you go *NINE* THOUSAND? *TAKES* NINE.

*YES!* And *NOW* TEN." In a deep, emphatic growl at once encouraging and pleading. 'TEN *THOUSAND* DOLLARS.

"*YES!* And *NOW* ELEVEN."

Perry was prowling between the two spotters standing beside the two tables where the two now-determined bidders – determined *donators* – were seated, arms folded. Their attempted poker faces didn't, for a second, hide their anxious excitement. The crowd had punctuated every confirmed "thousand" since Ernie's first and roared approval to his every *"YES!"* With the contest now down to two, the auction of the football became its own football game. Each bidder and his spouse, their whole table, and their spotter pulling together as a team; fans on each side wildly cheering their own. Ernie Perry was referee. I was pacing back and forth on stage like a caged… panther? How do team owners sit in those skyboxes so stoically?

"*ELEVEN* THOUSAND. Will you bid *EE-LEVEN-THOUSAND-DOLLARS*?

"*ELEVEN!* And *NOW* TWELVE."

The crowd was coming unglued.

"Will you bid *TWELVE*-THOUSAND-DOLLARS?"

Suddenly, no immediate hand.

"I have ELEVEN and *NOW* TWELVE. Will you *GO* TWELVE?"

Neither bidder bit.

"Don't *leave* me now," Ernie pleaded.

"And *YES*! NOW *THIRTEEN*."

The bidders had just taken a breath.

"Takes *THIRTEEN* to be able to go. *YES!*"

But a short one.

"*THIRTEEN* and now *FOUR-TEEN-THOUSAND!* Have THIRTEEN and *NOW* FOURTEEN. Will you go… Y*ESSS*! And now *FIFTEEN-THOUSAND!*

"Have *FOURTEEN* and now *FIFTEEN* will you go FIF-TEEN-*THOUSAND*-DOLLARS on the football? *EEEYYYEEEESSSS!*"

What comes after "unglued"?

"And *NOW* SIXTEEN! I have FIFTEEN and *NOW* SIXTEEN. Don't *LEAVE ME* NOW. SIXTEEN THOUSAND.

"Have FIFTEEN and *NOW* SIXTEEN. Will you go SIXTEEN-*THOUSAND*-DOLLARS and make a *GREAT* donation tonight to Make-A-Wish?"

Ernie was encouraging, cajoling, "Will you go SIXTEEN-*THOUSAND*-DOLLARS?" egging them on. "It may be what puts us over the top. Have *fifteen* and now *sixteen*. Will you *go* sixteen?"

The last remaining bidder remained silent. Ernie turned right to him. "I have fifteen," he said. And with a gently taunting glance back toward the lead bidder, "He probably won't bid again at sixteen. Say 'yes' at *sixteen*-thousand-dollars."

No "yes."

"Sixteen-*thousand*-dollars."

No reply at all.

"I have him at *fifteen* and now *sixteen*," Ernie said, as he turned from the bidder in the lead to the bidder on the fence. "Takes *sixteen* to bid."

Still no bid.

Ernie Perry will push for every penny there is to be donated, but he knows where "too far" is, and he won't push past it.

"I have fif-teen-*thousand*-dollars. To bid takes *sixteen*. And now…"

With a big slashing motion of his left arm: "*OOONCE!*"

The ballroom gasped. The crowd was hoping.

"I have you at *fifteen* thousand. I'm asking a donation of *sixteen*-thousand-dollars.

"*TWWWICE!*" Bigger slash of the arm.

In less than ninety seconds of bidding, a football – with the scribbles on it of half a hundred men – was going to snag fifteen thousand dollars. Three kids' wishes granted right there.

"*And a half?*" rang out one more desperate Perry plea. "*Fifteen-five?*" – to the bidder who went fourteen thousand dollars but was going no further.

Silence. It was over.

Ernie raised his arm for his final slashing "*SOLD!*" He was facing the room, turned to his right, still imploring he who had surrendered. He couldn't see Kevin Donnalley walking toward him from his left. I could.

"Ernest… Ernest…"

Perry turned to me, and I nodded toward Donnalley, who leaned in to Ernie with a whisper. Perry turned to the bidder who had held at fourteen. "Sir, I've got *him* at fifteen thousand. Kevin says he'll get another one if *you'll* go fifteen thousand too."

On stage, above the crowd, I saw the nod and couldn't hold back, "WHOA!" as Ernie bent his knees and wound up a final slashing, "*EEYYYYEESSSSS!*"

An explosion to rival Panther Stadium on a Sunday. Shrieks shot through the ballroom; people leaped from their seats, pumping fists in the air.

"*THIRTY-THOUSAND-DOLLARS* HERE TONIGHT!"

Thundering applause.

"*FIFTEEN!*" Ernie said, pointing left, "and *FIFTEEN!*" pointing right.

"God bless you all!"

# CHAPTER 26

# ONE HUNDRED FIFTY-FIVE

BACKSTAGE, the money counters were counting madly. They totaled the take from the auction, along with the night's ticket sales and a separate, lower-priced silent auction, and were getting ready to roll it up with all that had already been raised from Hope charms and hot chocolate drives, to deferred vacations and returned Christmas presents, to Panther tickets auctioned on the radio, to straight-ahead donations from one dollar to a hundred thousand. It would take a few minutes to have a grand total to announce. A million dollars was needed to officially grant Hope's wish, and the frenetic tabulating was for real. A lot of money had been raised in the four weeks since Hope had launched us on a 50,000-watt journey into the limitless possibilities of a faith-filled child's mind. Pushing three quarters of a million dollars, I had heard, and there had been no secret sandbagging. No one knew if the million would be reached even now.

I introduced Amy Laws, Director of Wish Programs for Charlotte Make-A-Wish. She, too, was there when Hope officially made her wish and worked most closely with her to make it come true. Amy deals with seriously sick kids every day, and she is serious about seeing their wishes granted – and granted right. That's what makes the kids' dreams come true. And Amy's. She's given her life to kids and their wishes.

"In 1980 there was a little boy named Chris Greicius who had a simple wish," she began. The storyteller stood elegantly in black velvet with shoulder-length blonde hair pulled back on the sides, the Hope charm around her neck.

"He wanted to be a police officer. With the dedication of his mother and the Phoenix, Arizona police department, his wish came true. Chris's wish was the inspiration from which Make-A-Wish was born. A couple of days after his wish was granted, Chris lost his battle with leukemia. Chris's mother Linda is with us tonight."

Warm, welcoming applause and cheers.

"This is the Celebration of Hope…the celebration of Hope's life," Amy continued, "and now her memory. Everything in this room tonight was by Hope's approval… from the linens, to the music, to the Rat Pack theme. The whole nine yards. A special part of this room is the stars. Along the walls you see the balloons, and from the balloons hang stars, and on those stars are the names of the 155 children Hope had in mind when she said she wanted to help grant their wishes."

How had I not figured that out?

"And some of those wishes have already come true. Like Jamal's. He had a simple wish for a shopping spree, which came true in December.

"There is Lindsay, who wanted to dance with Cinderella. On Christmas Eve, she and her family were seated at the royal table in the Magic Kingdom at Cinderella's Castle. After dinner, she and Cinderella had the first dance. And then there is Amber Ashworth, who is with us tonight. Amber, where are you? There you are!"

Laws sighted Amber in the crowd, and with love gleaming from her eyes, pointed to her.

"Stand up, Amber."

Happily, but shyly, Amber consented to a room full of applause that carried the warmth of the sun, gently turning back and forth in place to cover the self-consciousness she felt standing before the crowd. She wore a large black shawl over her dress; a soft, oversized, light-pink bowler hat that preciously, but not entirely, hid her bald head; and she was wearing a Hope charm. She didn't stand solo for long.

The room full of partiers still jazzed by the auction and anxious for a total – and ready for the band and a night of dancing – returned to their seats and listened in rapt silence.

"Amber also suffers from osteosarcoma," Amy revealed, her eyes reflecting the hurt in her heart the instant she said the words, "and she and her family set sail on December 22 for a very magical Christmas together."

The whole room felt the hurt in its heart and the irony of the moment. Hope was gone, but Amber, battling the same cancer, was there; her wish granted because of the granting of Hope's.

"That's what we're all about. Those are the types of wishes we grant. And I was asked to speak about the impact of Hope's wish, but…"

She paused, then swallowed before continuing. "There really is no way to measure the impact.

"Because how do you measure the impact of a child who gave up her babysitting money to Make-A-Wish? How do you measure the impact that'll have on her life when she grows up? Or all the children we heard about over the holidays who asked their parents to take their Christmas presents back and donate the money to Make-A-Wish because they had heard about Hope? Very special to me are our own wish children who have had their own fundraising efforts. Jim and Lisa Wright from Rockingham are here with their daughter, Abby, who met the Wiggles a couple of months ago."

Jim stood, carrying in his arms his 4-year-old daughter who was barely bigger than a baby. Abby suffers from a rare, life-threatening form of dwarfism.

"They have already raised over a thousand dollars and are planning a large benefit in February.

"And," Amy said, beaming, "I was just handed a check by one of my favorite wish children, Evan Harbison... who met Michael Jordan in March... a check for nine thousand dollars! Thank you very much."

To loud cheers, Amy proudly waved a poster-sized check over her head made out to Make-A-Wish with 'Hope Stout' in the memo line.

"Evan's here tonight with his parents and his brother. I asked Evan to be my date, but," Amy grinned, "he blew me off.

"When we talk about wishes and we see these kids, they inspire us to continue doing this until there's a cure for cancer and every other childhood disease; to bring hope and strength and joy to these kids when they need it most."

The applause for Amy seemed to last several minutes. Then I was back onstage one final time.

"All right. We're ready to see a number. Ready to make a little noise, and then bring the band out?"

I called Stuart and Shelby, and everybody from the Stout family, to the stage – including Hope's 6-foot-5 date.

"Total as of now... Gimme a countdown!

"THREE..."

*The entire room was standing and shouted along with me.*

"TWO..."

*When there's a hurt, everyone hurts; when there's a celebration, everyone celebrates.*

"ONE!"

*The crack of a drum, and...*

Screams shot through the room as the throng saw the numbers start zipping onto the video screens under a headline declaring "The Power of a Wish."

"One Million…

"One hundred sixteen thousand…

"Eight hundred thirty-nine!"

Hope's wish, granted. One hundred fifty-five others would be.

MOLLY GRANTHAM, in a shimmering black gown, was at the celebration and was on the air live from the ballroom seconds later with the breaking news. She was the lead story at eleven o'clock with a full report.

Saturday morning, the banner printed above the fold – above the masthead even – of the *Charlotte Observer*, declared:

## HOPE'S WISH IS GRANTED!
### Make-A-Wish drive tops $1 million

Don Hudson had been there. His headline said it all:

## IT WAS A FINE NIGHT IN THE CITY OF HOPE

And it was. It was sublimely fine. A lot of amps are pumped through the millions of lights that adorn the buildings uptown every night, but I doubt Charlotte has ever shone brighter.

Two nights later in Philadelphia, the Panthers beat the Eagles 14-3. Cinderella would be going to The Ball.

THE DAY BEFORE THE SUPER BOWL, yet another story appeared in yet another newspaper about Hope. It told about kids sending in their allowances, and about the funds being raised. It told of her special friendship with Kevin Donnalley, of the Celebration of Hope, and of the crazed auction of the two footballs. It said the money raised had risen to over $1.2 million. The story said Donnalley had fought in the trenches of the NFL for thirteen seasons and watched teammates play through bone-jarring injuries, but he'd never seen a greater example of courage than the freckle-faced, 12-year-old from Weddington, North Carolina, Hope Stout.

There had been countless stories published and broadcast about the girl and her wish and her Panther. That one ran in the *New York Times*.

LATER THAT YEAR, the Monday after Thanksgiving, I talked on the show with another little girl. She had just turned four years old. She had Wilms' tumor, a childhood kidney cancer. She was in the Bahamas with her parents and brother and had just been swimming with the dolphins.

"He kissed me," she laughed.

Emma Banks was number One hundred fifty-five.

<br>

The End

# EPILOGUE

The Spirit of Hope Keeps Rocking On

ADAM VINATIERI'S KICK sailed 41 yards toward the end zone as the final four seconds of Super Bowl XXXVIII ticked off the clock. When it cleared the goal posts, nine cannons exploded as one blasting clouds of confetti into the air pronouncing the end of the game, the end of the NFL season, and the end of the dream for the Carolina Panthers. They had been Cardiac to the end, the Cats. They scrambled back from the wrong side of a 21-10 fourth quarter score to tie the juggernaut-of-the-decade New England Patriots 29-29 on a Jake Delhomme touchdown pass to Ricky Proehl. A fluke duck-hook kickoff by John Kasay went out of bounds and jump-started the Patriots to their 40-yard line, but a great kick probably wouldn't have made much difference. A minute, eight seconds on the clock was being too generous to future Hall of Famer Tom Brady. He completed four straight passes to march into comfortable field goal range. The 37 points the Panthers and Patriots scored in the fourth quarter is still a Super Bowl record, just as Jake's 85-yard touchdown pass to Muhsin Muhammad, with less than seven minutes left, is still the game's longest. It was one of the great Super Bowl games of all time, and the Panthers almost won. But no one much remembers.

During the halftime show, there was a little problem with Janet Jackson's outfit.

THE PANTHERS WALKED back to their locker room under Houston's Reliant Stadium, silent to a man. Inside, John Fox stood in their midst.

"It was a great ride, men, and you fought your asses off. You've got nothing to be ashamed of.

"I know you're hurting right now. I'm hurting too. But don't anybody walk out of here with your head down. You've got a lot to be proud of."

Those weren't idle words. Those 53 guys had taken a season that seemed in the tank halfway through the first game and had come within one kick of winning it all against a team that was defining itself as one of the NFL's dynasties. The league and the sports media, and even a lot of fans, may not have given them much of a chance, but the Panthers themselves had always seen it differently. To everyone else they were Cinderella, wondrously whisked to the ball by the wave of a magic wand, but they believed they belonged at the dance. They had come to believe they belonged there because from the start, John Fox had seen them there. In only his second season as head coach, Fox's win-by-not-losing, use-the-running-game-to-drive-the-offense, and live-off-the-defense formula, and his one-hundred-percent belief in his team – which became their belief in themselves – had taken the Panthers all the way to the Super Bowl.

The NFL's most dominant team of the decade had simply danced three points better than Cinderella.

KEVIN DONNALLEY SAT for a long time on a chair in front of his locker, elbows on his knees, face hidden in his hands. He knew what was coming. There being no way to avoid it, he finally raised his head in surrender, and as slowly as he could while still doing it, pulled off his big number 65 jersey; then his massive shoulder pads. He sat some more, in his sweat-drenched, sleeveless T-shirt with four-inch numerals "58" and "51" on the front.

Donnalley gave himself two weeks to get over the hurt of losing the Super Bowl. Two weeks to get over the pounding pain that came with every game. Two weeks to see if he might change the decision he had made before the start of his thirteenth season. The hurt and the pain didn't last, but the decision would. On Monday, February 16, 2004, Donnalley called a press conference at Panther Stadium and announced his retirement.

"The camaraderie, the locker room," is what he told the reporter who asked what he would miss the most. "The guys."

"It's such a tough job, people can't even imagine, but doing it with a great group of guys, and then when you have some success, you can't think of a better feeling."

Donnalley did have some success over his thirteen years in the NFL, winning everything but a Super Bowl ring in his last. And what was the highlight of it all, another reporter asked?

"Being able to meet a girl like Hope Stout. To get to know her and build a relationship and get to know her family."

Donnalley retired from football. There would be no retiring from Hope.

Jeff Mitchell played two more seasons in the NFL, both with the Panthers, before retiring at age 31. When he was only 34, his left hip had to be replaced. Collateral damage from eight seasons of crouching his 6-foot-4-inch, 300-pound frame down to the ground, snapping the ball through his legs to quarterbacks, and exploding upward into mortal combat with charging 330-pound defensive linemen. In 2011, it had to be replaced again.

Jennoris "Jeno" James and Todd Steussie both left the Panthers in the months after the Super Bowl. James played three more NFL seasons, Steussie, four. James played his final three years with the Miami Dolphins. Steussie played two years for Tampa Bay and two for St. Louis.

Mitchell, James, and Steussie never made it back to the Super Bowl. Jordan Gross is still trying. The 2012 season was his tenth in the NFL. He has been named to the Pro Bowl twice, is the senior member of the Carolina Panthers' offensive line, and is one of the captains of the team. He, along with star receiver Steve Smith, are the last members of the Super Bowl Panthers still playing for the team.

The Panthers slipped to 7-9 after their Super Bowl season but bounced back the year after that and made it to the 2005 NFC Championship Game. They were manhandled by the Seattle Seahawks. Over the next five seasons, they had only one winning year. In 2008, they finished 12-4 and entered the postseason with promise. In their first-round playoff game, at home in Charlotte, Jake Delhomme threw five interceptions and fumbled the ball away once in a miserable 33-13 loss to Arizona. The Panthers lived a long off-season with those memories. Jake, especially, was chomping at the bit for opening game 2009, at home, against the Philadelphia Eagles. He threw four interceptions and gave up a fumble in a frightening 38-10 loss that launched his worst year in the NFL.

Jake Delhomme was cut by the Panthers after the 2009 season. The team had to pay the $12 million left on his contract. At his farewell news conference, the tears made it clear that money may buy security, but not immunity from the blow of being dumped. Jake was picked up as a backup for the Cleveland Browns in 2010, but didn't see much action. In November 2011, an injury left the playoff-bound Houston Texans in need of a number two quarterback. They signed a 36-going-on-13-year-old veteran who was still an enthusiasm epidemic.

Delhomme only played in one game all year. It was the last game of the season and the last game of his career.

On his final drive in the National Football League, Jake passed for a touchdown.

John Fox never put together back-to-back winning seasons as head coach of the Panthers. He was cut loose by Jerry Richardson the year after Delhomme but was quickly hired as head coach of the Denver Broncos. In his second season, 2012, he came within one game of going to the Super Bowl again.

Mark Fields beat his Hodgkin's disease and returned to the Panther lineup for the 2004 season. He played in fourteen games and was named to the NFL Pro Bowl team. Just before the 2005 season, the Hodgkin's returned. Fields beat his cancer a second time, but he never played again in the NFL.

In front of Panther Stadium, there is a large bronze statue of a man, small in size, but giant in stature. He is wearing his football uniform and holding his helmet. Determination on his face, commitment in his eyes, you sense his calm, quiet strength beyond the chiseled metal. Sam Mills kept pounding against cancer and kept coaching linebackers for the Panthers through the 2004 season. He died at his home in Charlotte the morning of April 18, 2005. He was 45. The Panthers retired his number 51, but it is still a common site in the stadium on Sunday afternoons in the fall.

DURING THE 2003 SEASON, more than 200,000 "Drop the Hammer on Cancer" wristbands were sold. Team reps aren't certain how many 58-51 T-shirts and towels were bought by fans, but the number was large.

In 2004, the Drop the Hammer campaign was renamed "Keep Pounding" in the spirit of Sam Mills' emotional speech to the team before the playoff game against Dallas. "Keep Pounding" key chains were added. More than 200,000 sold.

The "Keep Pounding" campaign continues through game day efforts and donations. It has raised $1.4 million for cancer research, patient support, and survivor programs through Carolinas Medical Center where Sam, Mark, and Hope were treated.

And that cool black T-shirt that sold like funnel cakes at a state fair during the playoff run with the faces of Donnalley, Mitchell, Steussie, James, and Gross surrounding a snarling panther, FAT CATS in team-blue across the top and CAROLINA'S SPECIAL BREED at the bottom? There was something else printed on it: IN MEMORY OF HOPE STOUT. It was Jeff Mitchell's idea. He designed it and did the leg work.

"It's something we wanted to do in memory of Hope," Mitchell said. All the Fat Cats, and in fact, the whole Panther locker room, John Fox later said, had been grabbed by her. The proceeds went to Make-A-Wish.

THE STOUTS ARE A FAMILY of supreme faith, and right up to the second she died, Hope expected she would be healed. So did Stuart and Shelby, Hope's sisters, and everyone else.

"Dying is not an option," Stuart told himself from the moment of her diagnosis.

"We are *not* just letting nature take its course," Shelby vowed the minute she heard Dr. McMahon suggest that some parents of children in Hope's dire straits might.

"Cancer will not beat this kid. She is too tough," Stuart's close cousin, Wendy Reeder, had declared, grabbing his face and pulling it close to hers that day in the hospital when they had all gathered to hear the news.

Hope, herself, had said quite matter-of-factly on the video for the Celebration, speaking of her own desire to be on a TV show, "I want my wish after I'm better."

If ever a family of a seriously ill child had one-hundred-percent faith in God, it was theirs. The Stouts believed, and they prayed with certainty, that He would take away Hope's cancer. They prayed for and expected a miracle, and along their journey, they had seen signs from God telling them they would get it: like the revelation of the "Hope Window" to Shelby in the hospital chapel.

Yet from the time she was diagnosed, Hope's condition never did anything but worsen. For all their faith and prayers and seeing of signs, there was never anything but more charging cancer behind any light they thought they were glimpsing at the end of any tunnel.

So to what end, faith? The Stouts had put it in God's hands, and the faith and prayers that did not cure Hope's cancer, also did not keep their hearts from cracking, or their fears and frustrations from boiling over. Hope had her moments, like her crutches-slinging breakdown over the bad news of September 24 and the prospect of yet another horrible round of treatment. Shelby's aching desperation in the hospital vestry was not a singular incident. And reality punched Stuart out many times, like the evening of October 30.

For Holly's sweet-sixteenth birthday, barely ten days after Hope's miraculous weekend of candy, football, and meeting a football player, Stuart was fervidly looking forward to taking the birthday girl and Shelby and Hope out for a belly-busting dinner and decadent desserts at the Cheesecake Factory, a family favorite. He came buoyantly home from work to find three of his FOURCHIX (Austin was at college) in the den, tears streaming.

Hope was in excruciating pain. They didn't know it, but the cancer in her knee was back on the rampage, having been more patient than VP-16 was powerful. It pressed mercilessly inside her. There was no way she could go to dinner. As Hope cried in pain, Holly cried for her suffering sister and perhaps, secretly, for her special birthday, spoiled. Shelby cried for Hope, for Holly, and for her family's helplessness.

The sight of his girls so broken, his vision of their night so suddenly shattered, was just too much. Stuart lost it. He charged into the garage. Before he knew it, he was holding a hammer and storming out into the darkness of the night and their amply wooded back yard.

It was a random act of violence. That particular pine tree was an innocent victim. If indicted, Stuart would plead temporary insanity, and the jury would find him not guilty by reason of who in the world could blame him.

He bashed the hammer into the trunk of the tree over and over and over. With all of his might and misery and anger released into his right arm, elbow, and hand, Stuart raised the weapon into the air and slammed it savagely home again and again. He pummeled the bark until it was bloody with tree sap and the wood underneath riddled with deep contusions. As he flailed away in his hammering fury, Stuart shouted his rage.

"I'VE HAD IT, GOD! *You and me are done. Do you hear me?* You aren't listening, are you? Why aren't you healing this kid? WHAT HAS SHE DONE TO DESERVE THIS?

It's time for YOU to start listening to US. We are praying constantly, and so is everybody else! *Enough of this! HEAL THIS CHILD!*"

Stuart had so emptied himself onto that poor pine that after several minutes of manic hammering, he all at once hurled the thing deep into the woods and crumpled like a milk carton to the base of the tree and cried. He was spent, helpless. Dragged eventually by reluctant feet back into the house, Stuart was as startled by what he saw then as he was when he had arrived home a half-hour earlier, ready for a birthday party: smiles on the faces of his CHIX.

Shelby, Holly, and Hope had emptied themselves too. They, too, were entirely spent. But they had surrendered to their helplessness and had fallen into a prayer that God would, in that moment, ease Hope's pain and soothe their hearts. Relief was almost instant. Hope's hurt seemed to lift right out of her, and they all felt a peacefulness wash over them. As soon as Stuart saw his girls' faces, the peace that had filled them warmed right through him.

There is a song sung by Scott Krippayne that is a Stout family favorite. "Sometimes He Calms the Storm, and Other Times He Calms His Child."

Back when he had taken Austin to North Carolina State for orientation, Stuart found himself in a small group session for parents of incoming freshman where he had the chance to talk with some other parents. He told the group about Hope's cancer and its effect on their family. Another man then revealed that his own daughter had battled and beaten leukemia. Stuart connected with his fellow traveler and was joyful hearing of the girl's victory, but then was rocked when the man said his marriage had become a casualty of his daughter's cancer. "I can almost guarantee your marriage will not survive this," the man had told Stuart.

Stuart and Shelby Stout's marriage did not become a casualty of their daughter's cancer. They remain intensely and thoroughly and happily together. Cancer did not claim their marriage, and it did not derail their other daughters. Austin graduated from North Carolina State and works in the Baltimore headquarters of Under Armour, the successful maker of popular athletic wear. Holly graduated from the University of South Carolina and is pursuing a career in photography. She is deeply involved in mission work.

The faith-full family was devastated. But not destroyed.

When their days were darkest and their challenges greatest, when their worst fears were realized and their horror most horrific, when their agony became most agonizing and frustration boiled into rage, faith brought peace. Every time they mourned, every time their spirit poured out, every time their aching hearts cried out – through unfathomable pronouncements in doctors' offices, through new realities thrust upon them obliterating the life they had known, through restless days and sleepless nights watching disease murder their little girl – when life left them battered and empty, God was there to fill them and carry them.

So to what end, faith? To this end, faith: it is the channel through which the Stouts were given what they needed to handle what life had given them which they could not handle themselves.

As for that stained glass window in the hospital chapel, it was a sign all right, but Shelby realized later that in her desperation and wanting that day, she hadn't taken the window in entirely. The redheaded girl in the glass was being healed, but she was glowing radiantly and wearing a white gown as she readied to cast off her crutches. She was standing with Jesus, the "Beloved Physician," at the gates of heaven.

She was healed by Him there.

I DIDN'T KNOW IT at the time, but the email that was waiting for me the morning of Tuesday, December 23, before my final show of 2003 – the one sent by a "friend of Hope" telling me she was sicker than people knew – had been sent by Danette Rutherford, the mother of Hope's best friend, Emily, and one of the conspiring sisters who had cooked up Hope's surprise meeting with Kevin Donnalley. The afternoon before, Monday, December 22, Danette had called Shelby and was stunned to learn how bad a turn Hope had taken after the film crew left on Saturday. She rushed over.

From inside the front door, Danette could just barely see Hope down the hall in the den where she was hooked to a steady morphine drip with a pump for the sudden surges of pain. She was having great difficulty breathing. It was frightening. Hope was worlds away from the girl Danette had seen on Saturday and had heard me talk with on Friday, and she thought I should know.

Emily had come to Hope's house with Danette. She and Hope were best friends who had laughed and played together since they were a spying Spice Girl and an M&M. She had been there when Hope met Kevin Donnalley, and they had laughed again at the film shoot just two days earlier. Though she had brushed out Hope's hair when it finally surrendered to the chemo, what was happening now was beyond any 12-year-old's frame of reference. Hope and Emily were each too afraid to see the other.

Emily Rutherford became an elementary education major at Appalachian State University in the funky little North Carolina mountain town of Boone. She leads a Bible study and speaks with calm conviction about what Hope taught her in life.

"I had to grow up fast. I had to figure out what I would lean on in hard times. Through Hope and her illness, I figured out what faith meant to me."

My invitation to the Christmas Eve vigil outside the Stout home had come from Nina Wheeling, mother of Gina Wheeling, the Ashley Olsen to Hope's Mary Kate, in big adventures and British accents since first grade. She said there was going to be an informal candlelight service outside the Stouts' home that evening to sing and pray and surround them with love. They didn't want to send an open invitation to the public, but wanted to invite me.

One hundred fifty or so candles shone through the darkness, one lit off another in that exponential way candles are lit on Christmas Eve. A voice for every candle carried "Silent Night" from the clearing in the woods out front where all had gathered, to the hearts of the family gathered inside in its own vigil. The front door opened. Stuart and Shelby, Austin and Holly crowded the doorway and gazed in amazement. They were greeted by Nina and Gina. Hope remained a few steps away in the hospital bed she couldn't leave. She knew who was at the door, and Gina could see the frame of the bed where she knew her best friend lay.

Gina Wheeling majored in journalism at the University of North Carolina-Chapel Hill. She did her internship – for Make-A-Wish. She did a little of everything for the organization, but especially liked helping grant wishes. She worked with Amy Laws. "Thinking of Hope, it felt like a full circle."

Emily, now 22, had been home on break a while back, and Gina, also now 22, had come over. Two beautiful young women with bright eyes and big smiles, still as curious as ever, but not quite so goofy, were ready to take on life just as Hope would have been – if cancer hadn't had other plans.

Shelby Stout was there too.

OVER THE FOUR WEEKS from the Friday morning I first started talking about Hope and her wish, to the Friday night of the big Celebration, a thought had occurred to more than a few people in the Carolinas. Many emailed me. Each made the point in their own way, but they made the same point still:

---

From: JC345@
Sent: Wednesday, December 24, 2003 12:04 PM
Subject: Hope needs Help

---

Keith,

I've been thinking. Where are the Bank of America, Wachovia, and Duke Power checks? The Panthers' organization could take care of the million dollars with one check. How about (Charlotte Bobcats owner) Bob Johnson? What's one million to a billionaire? Yes, they give to other organizations, but let's put a little heat on these folks.

---

So often that had been the Charlotte way. As Don Hudson had described it in a column, "Raise $500,000 and guilt the big banks and Duke Energy into paying the other half." What a blessing it never happened.

One hundred fifty-five wishes were granted, not because a financial hole needed filling, but because there was a wish in a little girl's heart. A couple of six-figure checks written without sacrifice by a couple of corporations could certainly have funded all the other kids' wishes, but that would have snuffed out the power of Hope's. Amy Laws knew that better than anyone. That's why when asked to speak about the impact of Hope's wish, her question was, *How do you measure the impact of a wish?*

Laws was the official Make-A-Wish representative on the agenda that night at the Celebration, and the impact question she was asked to speak on was a literal one. Slotted logically near the end of the program, it was a summing-it-up talking point before the final money total would be announced. The question quite naturally implied dollars and numbers and comparisons to other years in reply. But dollars and numbers and comparisons are merely the measurable. Amy Laws had helped grant hundreds of wishes over the years. She saw past the obvious and the measurable, to the profound and immeasurable.

Because, as Amy asked at the first Celebration of Hope, how would you measure the impact of a child who gave babysitting money to Make-A-Wish? How would you measure the impact that'll have when they grow up? Same for the children we heard about over the holidays who asked their parents to take their Christmas presents back and donate the money. How do you measure the impact on and through the lives of all the untold, unknown kids who took up collections, sold hot chocolate, or did anything at all to help raise a buck for Hope – or maybe raised no bucks at all just then but still had a seed, maybe as small as a mustard seed, planted inside them by Hope?

How would you measure the impact on and of other Wish Kids? Abby Wright, afflicted with exceedingly rare opsismodysplasia dwarfism; a tiny, beautiful girl sentenced to a wheelchair and ventilator but as full of life as any almost 4-year-old. Abby wanted her family to hold their own celebration to honor Hope and help Make-A-Wish in their hometown of Rockingham, and they did. Zach Ramsey had soft-tissue cancer that had quite oddly developed on his prostate when he was only fifteen. Hope's wish granted his, Panther season tickets. This intensely life-living, cancer-battling kid made fast friends of the bunch of thirty-somethings who sat near him each week in section 310. He turned them first into Make-A-Wish supporters, and then into supporters of the Zach Ramsey Children's Cancer Fund, the fund he started with his own money to help kids, and their families, battling cancer.

How do you measure the impact on and of Harley Wilson's family? Harley lived about one hundred miles northwest of Charlotte. His wish for a trip to Disney World had been granted the year before Hope made hers. He really loved that trip, especially the kiss he got from Cinderella. Harley had been born with lung disease and needed a double lung transplant. After a long time on a waiting list, he finally had a transplant and was two months down the road to recovery when the infection set in. Harley Wilson was ten years old, and his funeral was the same day and time as Hope's. His family asked memorials be made to grant Hope's wish. His proud, heartbroken uncle emailed to tell me.

Beyond Wish Kids, beyond families of kids whose wishes had been granted because of Hope's, beyond even kids at all – how do you measure the impact on a man who called John Hancock the night John played back the conversation with Hope? He said he was on a fixed income, but he wanted to give. He could only give five dollars; would that be okay? Could Make-A-Wish take a donation that small?

How do you measure the impact on a woman like Mary P? She wrote to tell me she was glad she had my show on in her office when I played the Nicole Nordeman "Legacy" song with clips of Hope from her conversation with me mixed in.

"I am a mother of three, married for 25 years, and feeling sorry for myself for where I am in my career," she said. "How quickly we forget as adults that the simple things are the most important, that simple faith does prevail, that all God wants from us is our hearts and a willingness to obey. I pray someday I, too, will leave a legacy of hearts and lives touched."

I received emails from hundreds of Mary Ps. Only the names and the specifics changed.

A year and a half's worth of funds were raised in 28 days because people responded to the wish of a child; to the love of God spoken through a dying girl's voice. Even the "elephant" that was bagged wasn't a billionaire basketball team owner. He was just a small businessman moved to do something far more than, by any typical measure, he should.

It was the *spirit* of Hope that granted her wish, grabbing people just as she had grabbed the football player and the radio guy.

The true impact of a wish is the change it brings in hearts that are grabbed by it.

A YEAR AFTER THE FIRST Celebration of Hope, a second was held. Kevin Donnalley and Jeff Mitchell were there. Todd Steussie's seat was taken by Steve Smith. During the auction, a behind the scenes tour of Panther Stadium – including locker room and training facilities with Jake Delhomme as the tour guide – became the hot item. The bidding had run into several-thousand-dollar territory. The showdown finally came at $12,000. Smith stood up, pulled out his cell phone, and called Jake. Ernie Perry cranked up that big slash of his arm and belted out his trademark *YESSS!* as each of two bidders bought a $12,000 date with Jake. The roar in the ballroom was like a warm hug from an old friend.

The Celebrations continued each January. Kevin Donnalley and Jeff Mitchell attended every one and Steve Smith several, along with other Panthers, current and former, including John Fox and Mark Richardson. Unique Panther prizes – like a complete Julius Peppers autographed uniform, from helmet to cleats, including jersey, pants, and gloves – were always the hit of the auction, which was always conducted by Ernie Perry. Each year Ken Lyon gave a soul-softening invocation, and Amy Laws talked of special kids and the power of wishes. Stuart and Shelby Stout thanked door-busting crowds for their support and thanked God for Hope. I hosted each one, joined after the first couple by Molly Grantham. They were a fabulous annual reconnection with Hope and her wish and the Panthers, prompted not by mere nostalgia, but by the relentlessness of cancer and other illnesses in putting kids on the Make-A-Wish list. Everyone felt Hope still wishing.

In 2009, the Make-A-Wish board decided to move in a different direction. Over its six years, the Celebration of Hope raised millions of dollars and funded hundreds of wishes. In the midst of their horrible nightmares, hundreds of kids were granted incredible moments and hundreds of families given indelible memories because of one little girl and the spirit of her wish.

THE DECISION TO CLOSE the door on the Celebrations was heartbreaking, but it opened a window. Hope had made another wish. She had hinted at it in our conversation when I asked her where the thought behind her wish had come from. She talked about how, when her mom would be with her in the hospital, Shelby "would go find out about the other kids and families who were in there and see what their story was."

"…I heard some of them were alone… didn't have their parents there because they had to work to pay off medical supplies…

"...I honestly cannot see myself fighting this cancer without my parents there... they have no idea how much they do...

"...the thought of some little kid who's younger than me, who could be going through something worse, alone, I want to do whatever I can to make their stay as good as it can be."

I was consumed by Hope's "grant all their wishes" wish, so it didn't click at the time, but beyond wanting to see wishes granted and being deeply upset about the other kids in the hospital, she had become concerned about their circumstances. She knew her family was doing okay despite the financial pressures of her illness. She had seen their expansive network of family and friends organize a golf tournament to raise additional money to help them through. She could also tell when she was seeing other families who weren't so fortunate. Her upset became outrage when she learned that one girl's mother had actually lost her job because of the time she was taking off work to be at the hospital with her seriously ill daughter.

"Children need their parents at the hospital with them! How could this happen?" she asked.

Following her mom's lead – just like when it was delivering meals to seniors or pitching in with Rainbow Express – Hope had begun saving the free cafeteria meal tickets and free parking passes staff would occasionally provide and gave them instead to other families who seemed like they needed the help. But that wasn't enough. She pressed; she wanted to do more. Shelby offered a deal. When Hope was healed, they would do something to help families who were struggling.

Shelby lived up to her pact with her daughter. She and Stuart formed the "March Forth with Hope Foundation" a few months after Hope died. It provides financial help to families of children battling cancer and other life-threatening illnesses. They have helped numerous families by covering housing and utility payments (often overdue), transportation costs and food, and various other expenses. The first money donated to the foundation was $18,000 the Stouts had left from the golf tournament that was held for them.

"March Forth with Hope Foundation." Hope was given to Stuart and Shelby on March fourth. It feels to them now like she left them with a command – *March Forth*. Another one of those profound visions and intriguing back stories we don't even know are there until they want us to.

The foundation throws a gala late each winter after football season. "Party planner" may not be the most common second career of former NFL players, but Kevin Donnalley carries the event on his big shoulders. He is a member of the Board of Directors of the March Forth with Hope Foundation. Two other foundation board members, Molly Grantham and I, team up as emcees. Amy Laws is always there.

The Carolina Panthers hosted the bash the first two years in the main concourse of the stadium with its stunning view of the field where Hope met Donnalley and the Panthers sprinted to the Super Bowl. Jeff Mitchell has faithfully attended each one. John Fox was at the first, but was moving to Denver by the time of the second. His replacement as Panthers' head coach was there, though. Ron Rivera made this new celebration of Hope and her wishes his very first public event after joining the team. With Donnalley and Mitchell present, along with Steve Smith and Jordan Gross, Rivera assured there would be Hope in the Panthers' future. During the auction, he jumped in with his own game tickets, field passes, and personal stadium tour. When Ernie Perry had coaxed the bidding into the thousands, and the standoff finally came...

The March Forth with Hope event has a main sponsor, United Spirit Corporation, a small company that puts on cheerleading competitions throughout the Southeast. It is owned by the same Jeff Fowlkes who delivered the cashier's check for $100,000 to the offices of Make-A-Wish after hearing Hope Stout on the radio.

It was unusual for Fowlkes to be in his car at that time of the morning. Hearing Hope, he was "shaken and shaking," he told me later. He felt God was trying to do something out of proportion through this little girl and felt stirred himself to do something out of proportion to help. He called his partners immediately. They were all in. A couple of hours later, he was at the bank.

Fowlkes and his organization have supported every Celebration of Hope and March Forth with Hope gala. He gives more than money. At the CHEERSPORT National Cheerleading Competition in Atlanta, the largest of its kind in the country, with nearly a thousand teams competing, the story of Hope Stout – a young cheerleader who made an out-of-proportion wish that changed lives – is always part of the program.

CHUCK COIRA WAS JUST ENDING his tenure with Make-A-Wish when I first talked with him about Hope that Friday morning, December 19. There was a reason he had come so close to breaking down so quickly that day. Yes, he had met Hope, had been grabbed by her in the way she grabbed people. And yes, he had been working with the Make-A-Wish team and the Stouts, and was emotionally invested in wanting to see Hope's wish granted. But Coira also knew something in a way that perhaps Stuart and Shelby hadn't yet accepted: Hope didn't have much time left.

Hope, herself, had been designated one of those "rush wishes." When Dr. Daniel McMahon was asked by Make-A-Wish for the standard medical clearance to go ahead with this wish of Hope's to grant the other kids' wishes – and for her to work to help raise the million dollars and plan her big Rat Pack Bash – he said, "Go ahead. Whatever she wants. But you'd better do it fast."

Amy Laws had relayed the urgency of the stark assessment to Coira. So there he was, on the phone, telling me and the Carolinas about this amazing girl, her out-of-this-world wish, and her commitment to it, and he knew she wasn't going to make it. He knew she might not even make it to the party she was helping plan. Coira was also telling me about Hope telling him that her cancer was "a gift from God," that without it she "would never ever have the opportunity to be able to touch so many other people's lives." This 12-year-old girl brutally battered by cancer and chemo had looked into the 54-year-old eyes of Chuck Coira and told him *he* should never feel sorry for *her*. Of course, he was on the verge of busting up from the moment he came on the air to talk about her. He'd been on the verge of busting up from the moment he'd met her.

Chuck Coira is an almost-retired representative for private-label jewelry manufacturers. Though his wife is the executive minister of a prominent Baptist church in Charlotte, he says he has "never been much of a religious man," but meeting Hope Stout caused a "seismic shift" in his life. His heart opened up, Coira says.

"I truly believe when I met Hope, I looked into the eyes of an angel."

ABBY WRIGHT BEAMED from her wheelchair during the "Celebration of Hope" she and her family threw in Rockingham, about ninety minutes from Charlotte, a few weeks after the big event at the Westin. It was a down-home barbecue and gospel-music bash attended by hundreds. Shelby and Holly Stout went on their way back to Charlotte from a weekend at the beach. Kevin Donnalley drove Stuart and me. Molly Grantham came and brought her dad. He had followed Hope's story and learned about Abby, and he lived not far from Rockingham. A special guest in attendance was Amber Ashworth, Abby's fellow Wish Kid, who'd also been at the first Celebration in Charlotte.

Abby is one of only four kids with opsismodysplasia dwarfism alive today. When she was born, doctors said she might live a few years. She turned fourteen years old in March. Abby's family almost lost her in 2008, when breathing difficulties left her unconscious for six months, and finally led to a long-feared tracheotomy. She rebounded, though, and today is doing better than ever. Abby's still only as tall as a toddler, but is very much an almost 14-year-old in every way but size. She's able to stand a bit now, and the ventilator she was once restricted to is needed only at night. Abby speaks but had been taught sign language when she was younger because it was feared that she someday may not be able to. She now signs songs of faith and strength for her church. Watch her here: www.abbywright.com.

Abby has never, not even once, asked "Why?"

Amber Ashworth died May 13, 2004. Her young body was finally forced to surrender to the same heartless, relentless osteosarcoma that claimed Hope.

She slipped away about nine in the morning having softly, and with a smile, told her family, "I love you," the night before.

ON TRYON STREET just south of Trade Street in the heart of uptown Charlotte, is the old Johnston Building. Dwarfed by glass and steel structures today, its sixteen stories made it the tallest building in Charlotte when it opened in 1924, with its beige brick and concrete, arched picture windows and doorway, and classic bronze-filled bank lobby entryway still in use today. On the tenth floor is the Charlotte Make-A-Wish office. It is far more functional than fancy. A sign at the unstaffed reception desk asks, "Please Ring Bell." Papers and boxes, envelopes and flyers, posters for events, and just plain stuff is everywhere. Down the hall to the left of the well-used conference room is a corner office once filled with pictures of kids.

*Filled* with pictures of kids, the office was. Scores of pictures of scores of kids – some in frames but most not – were taped and tacked to walls and bulletin boards, piled in stacks, and stood on book cases and book shelves. The desk stuck in the far corner was covered, too. It looked to have been backed into that corner by all the pictures. One needed not ask to know the pictures were of Wish Kids.

For several more years, Amy Laws granted wishes – into the thousands of wishes – but she didn't keep track except to figure it roughly when a writer pressed. Numbers are merely the countable; wishes are about kids, and Wish Kids are profound. Each one of the kids whose wishes Amy Laws helped grant, became a part of her. It took its toll. She feels bad that she almost always cried when she talked about kids and wishes. She shouldn't. Everyone who knows her loves that about her. Amy's was not the kind of job you left at the office. It filled the heart and broke it all at once, times thousands. Over the years, she'd thought about taking a different job in Make-A-Wish, or in darker moments, about quitting altogether.

At the end of May 2012, Amy finally did leave Make-A-Wish after all those years. The pictures of the kids went with her.

MOLLY GRANTHAM BECAME an Emmy Award-winning reporter known for coverage of gangs and revolving-door criminal courts in Charlotte. In 2010, she was named main co-anchor of WBTV's 5:30 and 11:00 p.m. news. She has never stopped telling Hope's story or the stories of many other kids with cancer and their wishes of so many kinds. She has reported on and helped the Panthers grant wishes, and she even brought Jordan Gross to visit a seriously ill child in the hospital. She helped a girl with cancer meet Justin Bieber, and she also saw Emma Banks and her family off at the airport on Emma's trip to swim with the dolphins. Molly has become the host of the annual Susan G. Komen Foundation "Race for the Cure," which draws 25,000 to uptown Charlotte the first Saturday morning every October. Her grandmother was a breast cancer survivor. Her mom beat breast cancer once but has recently had a recurrence and is still fighting. The disease killed her great-grandmother. Molly's dad was diagnosed with colon cancer a few months after he attended Abby Wright's "Celebration of Hope" in Rockingham. He lost his battle in 2006.

Molly has been a frequent player on my radio show. I did a "Week that Was" segment on her Friday night news for years, and we work together on projects that have grown out of each of us having been pulled into Hope's orbit. I help promote and also run in her Komen event. She emcees the charity motorcycle ride I hold each year. Hundreds turn out for the police-escorted ride and the barbecue and party afterward, which, thanks to generous WBT sponsors, gives one hundred percent of rider contributions to the families and kids we support. We ride for a specific child or two whose needs have come to our attention and divide the rest of our proceeds between the March Forth with Hope Foundation and the Zach Ramsey Children's Cancer Fund. I wish I could say the idea for the ride was mine. It came from my listeners.

Molly and I also co-host what has become a terrific event each fall in Charlotte, the "Give Back with Zach Tailgate Party." It benefits Zach's fund and is held at a casual banquet hall on the day of the Panthers' first away game each season. It has great support from the team with the Top Cats cheerleaders and Sir Purr attending, along with several former players. Kevin Donnalley and Jeff Mitchell happily humiliate themselves each year by leading the crowd in Panthers' cheers and dances before the game comes on.

EVERY YEAR AFTER THANKSGIVING, an email comes from the radio station program director asking me and the rest of the air staff what days we'll be taking off over the holidays. There are several of us, and scheduling fill-ins and backups for our producers, takes some planning.

From a little before Christmas until a few days after New Year's, I'll be taking off. This I know, and so does the PD; yet the point of the email is specifics. So flip open the calendar, check the actual holiday dates, factor in the official days off and the Saturdays and Sundays. Make plan, type email, hit send. Simple. Everybody does it or their own version. The process always sends the mind wandering to those last few working days of the year and the shows that will fill them.

We'll have four Christmas CD days this year. Jimmy Buffet and Chicago will be joined by "A Charlie Brown Christmas" CD day – when out of our breaks we'll play all the tracks from the TV special – and Juke Box Christmas CD day – when we'll play a mix of Christmas and holiday hits by Springsteen, Darlene Love, and other rock 'n' rollers.

We'll have year-end conversations with some old friends and regular guests. Bill Kristol and John Whitehead, maybe? Maybe. The years bring new old friends and many more guests. Molly Grantham will stop by. We'll talk about "The Year that Was." I'll do a thing we now wrap each week with, "Your Seven Seconds," where we crack open the 50,000 watts to callers in rapid-fire fashion for whatever comment on whatever topic they can pack into seven seconds before a buzzer goes off.

I'll riff out "My News and You are Welcome to It" to kick off each show, and we will, sometime in those last few days, absolutely have a chat with Doc Elmo accompanied by the playing of a couple of fabulous Christmas classics. On the last day, I'll have a few final, *no-doubt profound*, thoughts before giving Mark the cue to roll John Lennon's "Happy Christmas" and then exit stage left for a thirteen-day escape.

The last few shows of the year are pretty much mailed in.

But before those final, no-doubt profound, thoughts and that last hand cue for John Lennon, coming out of our 11:30 news, Mark will roll a tape. Big brass horns will blow the opening declarations of the carol "Joy to the World." As the string section joins in, I'll hear myself over the music…

"All right."

*With the slightest hesitation.*

"Keith Larson here."

*A touch of tentativeness.*

"And we have on the phone with us a 12-year-old girl who…"

*Only a toe in the water at first, but then I'll jump right in.*

"…had a big idea… as we've been talking about this morning."

And we'll be off to relive for the tenth time an eleven-minute and fifty-second conversation which I guess changed a few lives. One I know of for sure.

I will have gotten emails for weeks from people asking exactly what day we'll be playing back the conversation with Hope. They could listen any time they wanted right here: www.wbt.com/larson/thekids. A lot of people have told me, though, it works kind of like *A Charlie Brown Christmas;* there's something special about catching it the one time it's played on the air for everybody.

Soon as the tape is safely playing, I'll split the studio. It only takes those first few seconds, and sense memory rushes me right back into that surreal moment of years earlier. I know how it ends, and I end up in exactly that same place every time I hear it. Mark has to stay at the studio controls, just in case. When I walk back in twelve minutes later, he goes for a walk of his own.

As Hope Stout explains it all in her own words, opens up and reveals the timeless honesty in her heart and spirit with a passion and wisdom and insight that still doesn't seem like it could come from a 12-year-old, the phones at Make-A-Wish will ring once again with calls from people responding to the wish of a child; to the love of God spoken through a dying girl's bright, optimistic, young voice. The spirit of Hope keeps rocking on, which is a good thing.

There are now 326 kids on the Charlotte Make-A-Wish list.

# ACKNOWLEDGEMENTS

WHEN I SAT DOWN to begin writing That Season of Hope several years ago, I had no idea the hardest part would end up being the Acknowledgements. So many people's thoughts have gone into this book; so many thumbprints are on it. It's impossible to recognize everyone, fearing terribly understating anyone. So here goes, with apologies from the heart for any errors or omissions.

I could take a lot of space to detail her contributions or simply confess that the cover of this book could almost read, "By Keith Larson, with Nancy Larson *and* Molly Grantham." Thanks, Mol.

Kevin Donnalley, in addition to his general support, provided a resource without which this story simply would not be all that I hope it is. Kevin secured Head Coach John Fox's permission to discreetly roll videotape behind-the-scenes the entire 2003-2004 season. He provided his voluminous highlights for my review, putting me in the Panther locker room and team meetings, in players' homes, and on the road and on the field, for the entire season. Thanks, brother.

An important supporting resource was the book by Stuart and Shelby Stout, Hope's Wish, published by Thomas Nelson. It is their family's personal story about Hope's illness. For purposes of consistency, by mutual agreement with the Stouts and Thomas Nelson, certain facts and key quotes have been used here as they were originally reported in Hope's Wish. To learn more about Hope, and what she and her family went through, please read their story.

Thank you to literary agent Elizabeth Evans, who is not my agent, but who loved the story and read the manuscript multiple times and provided profoundly helpful direction. Thanks to Lee Ann with FirstEditing, and Janet Thoma, who was a help to the Stouts with their book and a help to me with mine.

Thanks to Charlotte Observer researcher Maria David – wow, the digging she did! – and to the Observer itself for permission to use articles and photos; the Carolina Panthers organization, especially Riley Fields, long-time radio voice Jim Szoke, and the Media Relations resources of Charlie Dayton; and WBT Radio/Greater Media Corporation and WBTV Television/Raycom Communications.

Thanks to people who were specifically interviewed for the book including the credit-deflecting Elizabeth Leland, the amazing Amy Laws, angel-seeing Chuck Coira, unlikely-and-unassuming-elephant Jeff Fowlkes, and Hope's best friends, Emily Rutherford and Gina Wheeling and their mom's, Danette and Nina. To countless people who contributed in friendship or conversation more so than "interviews" including Reverend Ken Lyon, Jeff Mitchell, Don Hudson, Bruce Mullan, and Jerry Gregory, and many other friends and members of the Stout family – especially Austin and Holly.

Though they never knew they were helping to write a book, I must thank the people of the Carolina's, and beyond, who actually made Hope's wish come true – especially the listeners of WBT Radio. As I say often on the air, the power of the 50,000-watts lies in the hands of the people who listen to the 50,000-watts.

Nancy and I, of course, want to thank our family – especially Matt, Hallie, and Kendall – for their support, particularly those times they didn't even know they were giving it. That's what family is about. And thanks to Kendall, specifically, for the cover design and graphic artistry.

Finally, to Stuart and Shelby Stout, my thanks go far beyond the matter of the substantial resource they were in the writing of this book. Because of them, and my producers Mark Thomas Seiler and Bo Thompson, I had a conversation with a young girl on my radio show on Friday, December 19, 2003. I hadn't seen her coming, but she changed my life.

She's still changing my life.

Author proceeds from the publication and sale of this book will be split between Make-A-Wish, The Carolina Panthers' "Keep Pounding" cancer foundation, and the March Forth With Hope Foundation

For more information:
www.ThatSeasonofHope.com
 That Season of Hope
@LarsonOffAir

# ABOUT THE AUTHOR

Keith Larson is the long time mid-morning personality at WBT AM/FM radio in Charlotte, NC and has been named among *Talkers Magazine's* "Heavy Hundred" Most Important Talk Hosts in the country three times. Before making the leap back into radio in 2000, he spent more than twelve years in marketing with McDonald's Corporation and Moroch, one of its largest advertising agencies.

Nancy Larson worked several years as an executive assistant before becoming a full-time Mom and homemaker. She has also spent the past 27 years as executive assistant to a career-hopping radio guy, marketing guy, writer guy.